W9-ASR-731

Build and Repair with Concrete

The Complete Do-It-Yourself Manual

Build and Repair with Concrete

The Complete Do-It-Yourself Manual

The QUIKRETE® Companies

The QUIKRETE® Companies
1790 Century Circle, NE
Atlanta, GA 30345

This book is dedicated to James Eugene Winchester, chairman of the board of The QUIKRETE® Companies, for his leadership, dedication, and vision in the packaged concrete industry.

A special thanks is also extended to all QUIKRETE® manufacturers for their much-needed help and cooperation in bringing this book to completion.

Preface

More and more of today's homeowners are taking an active role in the upkeep of their homes and property. And although the average do-it-yourselfer won't hesitate to pick up a hammer or paintbrush, a surprising number of people have the notion that concrete and masonry work is much too difficult and best left to professionals. The QUIKRETE® Companies have written this book to show that you don't have to be a professional mason to produce outstanding results with concrete. By using quality masonry products and following proven techniques, professional results can be achieved. Whether you want to lay a simple concrete slab, build an elaborate garden fountain, or repair a damaged concrete surface, this book will show you how to plan the job and how to complete it successfully.

Acknowledgements
We are grateful to the following organizations for their cooperation in pro-
viding photographs and other information for the book: Portland Cement
Association, The Brick Institute of America.

Library of Congress Cataloging in Publication Data

Build and repair with concrete.

    Includes index.
    1. Concrete construction—Amateurs' manuals.
I. QUIKRETE® Company.
TA682.42.B85   1986   693'.5   85-30139
ISBN 0-937558-16-8

Contents

SECTION II: REPAIR AND MAINTENANCE WITH QUIKRETE®

SECTION III: MATERIALS, TOOLS, AND PLANNING WITH QUIKRETE®

Introduction

Concrete is made by mixing four ingredients together in proper proportions: portland cement, fine aggregate (usually sand), coarse aggregate (usually gravel or crushed stone), and clean, potable water. A mix of cement, sand, and water, without the coarse aggregate, is called sand mix, and is used as a strong finishing or topping material in some projects and repairs.

Mortar mix consists of special masonry cement, fine sand, and other additives that provide the workability and stickiness needed when laying up brick, block, tile, etc.

The aggregates in concrete and mortar mixes are called inert ingredients, while the cement and water are known as active ingredients. When water is added to the mix, a chemical reaction (called hydration) between the water and the cement begins, causing the mix to harden. Hardening is caused by hydration, not the drying out of the mix. (Because concrete does not harden by drying out, it can harden even when submerged in water.) Because drying out could cause a drop in water content below the amount needed for the chemical reaction to work properly, concrete must be kept moist (cured) during the initial hydration process. Mortar used in masonry work is not normally cured in this manner, but it is equally important to use properly mixed mortar with the right working consistency. Like poorly cured concrete, mortar that is too wet or dry will give less than ideal results.

Concrete can be formed into practically any shape, with a variety of finishes, textures, and colors. Since it is made only of inorganic materials, concrete is impervious to decay, termites, and rodents. It is noncombustible, and when properly placed, concrete is usually not affected by heat and cold. These extraordinary properties combine to give concrete durability, good appearance, and long-term economy that few building materials can match.

The same desirable characteristics appear in masonry work as well. Hundreds of styles, textures, and sizes of brick, block, stone, tile, and specialty products allow amateur and professional masons to create and build thousands of practical, beautiful projects that will last not only for years, but for generations.

SECTION I:
QUIKRETE®
PROJECTS

What do a planter, a retaining wall, and a shuffleboard court have in common? They all can be made with QUIKRETE® masonry products. In this section, we'll show you how easy it is to make these as well as many other interesting and useful projects. From laying simple concrete slabs to building beautiful garden fountains, you'll learn step-by-step how to add beauty and value to your home and property. You can do it—with QUIKRETE®.

Layout Basics for Slabs and Footers

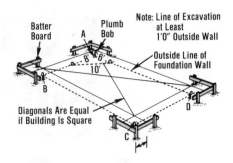

Note: Line of Excavation at Least 1'0" Outside Wall

The first step in placing large concrete slabs, patios, driveways, etc., is to stake out the area using the 3-4-5 triangular method. This method ensures square, true corners on square and rectangular surfaces, and any multiple of this ratio, such as 6-8-10 or 9-12-15, will give the same result. Always use a line level to ensure all lines strung are level. After staking out the area, double-check for squareness by measuring the diagonals between opposite corners. They should be equal.

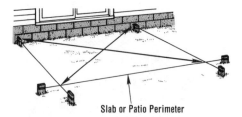

Slab or Patio Perimeter

When deeper trenches must be dug for wall and foundation footers, it is best to lay out batter boards. Batter boards are set back from the actual work area so they are not disturbed by digging and construction. They also serve as a record of all important locations, such as trench and footer dimensions and the location of the outer edge of the finished wall. To lay out batter boards:

1. Lay out the perimeter of the project by accurately driving stakes at the corners. About 5' outside these

stakes, drive 1" × 4" stakes and construct batter boards as shown. Because the trench must be at least 3' wide to allow room to work, batter boards should be 4' to 5' long.

2. Transfer the building lines to the batter boards by dangling a plumb bob over the outer edge of each corner stake while stretching a length of line between batter boards. This is best done as a two person operation.

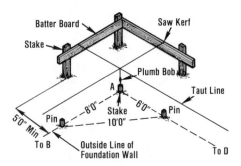

3. With the outside corner dimensions marked out on the batter boards, measure over the required distances to record the position of footer and trench edges. Cut small saw kerfs in

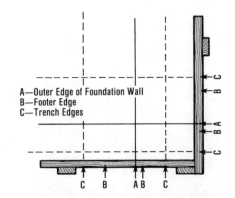

A—Outer Edge of Foundation Wall
B—Footer Edge
C—Trench Edges

the batter boards at these positions so that lines can be accurately strung and restrung whenever needed.

4. After digging the trench, a plumb bob can be used to transfer dimensions for footer forms and final wall positions.

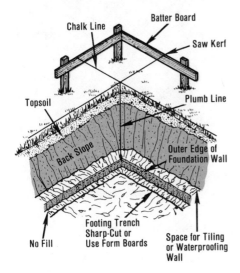

Concrete Sidewalks and Small Slabs

Tools and Materials

QUIKRETE® Concrete Mix
Gravel or crushed stone (if needed)
T square, measuring tape, mason's line, level, pickax, shovel, rake, tamper, hammer or half-hatchet, saw, screed, darby or bull float, hand float, finishing trowel, bricklayer's trowel, edger, and jointer
Forming lumber, stakes, and nails
Wheelbarrow and power mixer (recommended) or masonry hoe
Curing materials

Private walks leading to the front entrance of a home should be 3' to 4' wide. Service walks connecting to back or side entrances can be 2' to 3' wide. Sidewalks should be at least 4" in thickness, with a 4" to 6" range being most common.

Slope the walk away from buildings to provide proper drainage. A slope of 1/4" per foot is generally recommended, but check local codes and conditions.

Note: If you must work with concrete in hot or cold weather, be sure to read the precautions on page 154 before beginning.

SITE PREPARATION

1. Stake out the area for the walk or slab, using a T square, measuring tape, and twine. Use a line level to ensure proper placement and slope of lines.

2. Remove the sod and soil to the desired depth. Remember to account for the width of the forming lumber.

3. Nail and stake the forms in place. You may have to dig a slight trench to set the forms at the correct height.

4. Backfill against the forms to ensure stability.

5. Use the level to check for proper slope. Notice that when held level, the right end of the level is about 1/2" above the outside form, indicating a slight slope away from the building.

6. Tamp the subbase firm; then check for proper form depth, here 4". For larger jobs, or in areas of poor drainage, dig to a greater depth and add several inches of crushed stone or gravel to the base.

7. If desired, add wire mesh or rebar to the form bed, using small stones to elevate it above ground level.

MIXING AND PLACEMENT

1. Turn on the power mixer, add the QUIKRETE® Concrete Mix, and add water until the concrete mixes to a plastic-like consistency. Do not exceed mixer capacity. **Note:** QUIK-RETE® Concrete Mix can also be mixed manually in a wheelbarrow or mortar box.

2. Dampen the subgrade before making the pour. Note the use of a splash board to help direct the flow.

3. Spread the concrete throughout the form, working it in tight against corners and edges.

4. Strike off the concrete level with the top of the forms using the screed board. Fill in any low spots as you work. Several passes may be needed.

5. Float the concrete surface smooth, using a wooden or metal float or darby. Swing the tool in circles, holding the leading edge of the tool up slightly to keep it from digging into the concrete. Float the entire slab. Stop floating when the entire slab is fairly smooth and the float leaves no visible marks. All stone and gravel in the mix should have been worked below the surface.

6. Cut the concrete away from the forms by running an edging tool along the forms to compact the slab edges.

7. Using a straight piece of lumber as a guide, cut 1″ control joints into the slab every 6′ or so using a grooving tool.

Note: When a coarse finish is desired for non-slip footing, floating, edging, and grooving may be the only steps performed. When a denser, smoother finish is required, the surface is troweled once or several times with a stainless steel trowel. Troweling takes place after the surface moisture has evaporated from the surface and the concrete has lost its sheen. This setting time may vary greatly with weather conditions and the moisture content of the mix, from 30 minutes to several hours. Thirty minutes to an hour is average in most cases.

8. Once the concrete has set up, swing the trowel in the same circular pressing and polishing motion that was used in floating. Continue working until the surface is smooth and dense. You may wish to allow the concrete to continue to harden and then trowel once more for the densest possible finish. After troweling, redo edges and grooves.

9. Properly cure the concrete for 3 to 4 days. After the concrete has hardened sufficiently (48 hours or so) carefully remove the forms.

For Best Results

Use double head nails for easy form stripping.

Form curved forms using 1/4" plywood or kerfed lumber, or sheet metal.

Always make sure that the control joints are a quarter of the thickness of the slab.

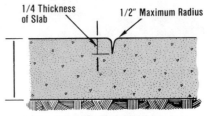

1/4 Thickness of Slab

1/2" Maximum Radius

Hand-Tooled Control Joint

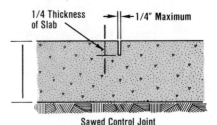

1/4 Thickness of Slab

1/4" Maximum

Sawed Control Joint

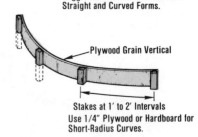

Smooth Inner Form Face

1/4" Plywood

2 x 4 Form

2 x 2 Stake

Suggested Detail at Joint between Straight and Curved Forms.

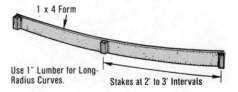

Plywood Grain Vertical

Stakes at 1' to 2' Intervals
Use 1/4" Plywood or Hardboard for Short-Radius Curves.

1 x 4 Form

Use 1" Lumber for Long-Radius Curves. Stakes at 2' to 3' Intervals

For long walks, install an expansion strip every 25′ to control cracking as the concrete expands and contracts with temperature and moisture changes. Expansion strip material is available at most hardware stores and is installed as follows:

1. Place a stop board across the form and then pour the slab.

2. Remove the stop board, place a length of expansion strip material against the hardened concrete, and then pour the following section of walk.

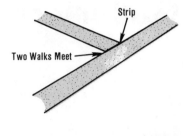

Two Walks Meet — Strip

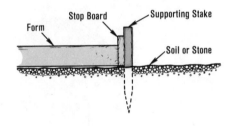

Form
Stop Board
Supporting Stake
Soil or Stone

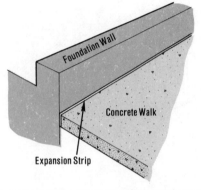

Foundation Wall
Concrete Walk
Expansion Strip

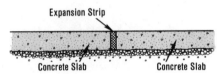

Expansion Strip
Concrete Slab   Concrete Slab

3. Expansion strips should also be installed where new walks or slabs abutt old walks, foundations, and walls, as shown in the following illustrations.

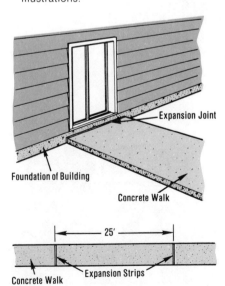

Expansion Joint
Foundation of Building
Concrete Walk

25′

Concrete Walk   Expansion Strips

Gallery of Slab Projects

Concrete slabs provide a strong, level base for countless items inside and outside the home. Here are just a few ideas to get you thinking.

Shuffle-board Court

Shuffleboard is a popular pastime for people of all ages, and with QUIKRETE® Concrete Mix it's easy to make your own shuffleboard court for your backyard.

You'll need a long, narrow area; an official shuffleboard court is 52′ long and 6′ wide, although it can be as small as 28′ long and 3′ wide.

Once you've chosen a good spot for the court, it is simply a matter of building the forms and pouring a concrete slab. Work the concrete with a steel trowel to produce a smooth, hard finish. When the concrete has cured for 3 to 4 days, coat the surface with a good concrete sealer; this will make the surface smooth enough to accommodate the wooden discs. When the sealer has dried, paint on the lines and numbers as shown in the illustration.

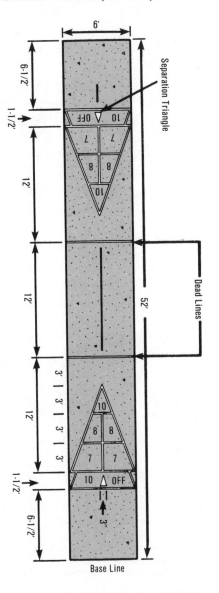

Footers for Walls

Regardless of the type of masonry material you are using to build the wall, concrete is the material of choice for the footer. A typical footer is twice the width of a wall and equal in depth to the wall's width. The footer should rest on a 6″ gravel base set below the frost line. Check with your local building department for the exact depth of the frost line in your area, and for any local specifications concerning the footer design for the job you have in mind.

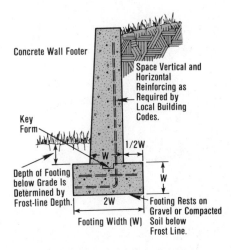

Concrete Wall Footer

Space Vertical and Horizontal Reinforcing as Required by Local Building Codes.

Key Form

1/2W

Depth of Footing below Grade Is Determined by Frost-line Depth.

W

W

2W

Footing Width (W)

Footing Rests on Gravel or Compacted Soil below Frost Line.

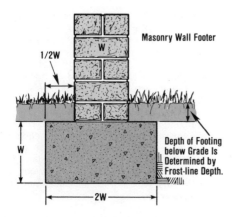

Masonry Wall Footer

1/2W

W

Depth of Footing below Grade Is Determined by Frost-line Depth.

2W

Tools and Materials

QUIKRETE® Concrete Mix
Gravel or crushed stone
Pickax, square-faced shovel, tamper,
  saw, screed, and level
Rebar, forming lumber, and stakes

CONSTRUCTING FOOTER FORMS

1. Lay out the footer location with batter boards as described on page 2. If the soil is firm enough to hold its shape when filled with wet concrete, consider making an earth form by digging to the correct depth and other dimensions with a square-faced shovel.

2. Firmly compact the soil using a tamper and add the 6″ gravel base to ensure good drainage.

3. Screed guides, leveled and staked at the correct height, will help in striking off concrete in earth forms. After the screeding pass, these guides are removed and the gaps filled with extra concrete and leveled with a trowel.

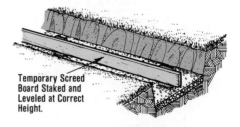

Temporary Screed Board Staked and Leveled at Correct Height.

4. In loose soils, construct strong wooden forms using sturdy lumber, stakes, and nails. Form boards must be parallel and level.

5. Place steel reinforcement bars 1/3 up from the base of the footer.

6. If the footer is to be the base of a poured concrete wall, install a keyway form as shown. This keyway will help tie together the footer and wall.

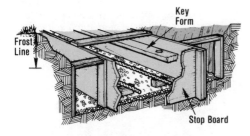

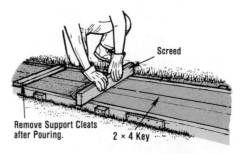

7. On slopes, construct a stepped footing to minimize the amount of concrete used. Stepped forms should rise no more than 2' per step and overlap at least 2' at each step. The same step principle can be used for earth forms.

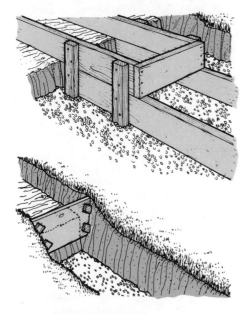

2. Screed the concrete level. If steel reinforcement is needed for the poured wall, insert it at this time. Predrilled holes in the keyway form make this an easy task. Remove the keyway form as soon as the concrete has set up sufficiently to hold its shape.

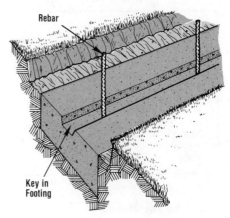

3. Cover the footer and allow it to cure for at least 3 to 4 days before removing forms and continuing work.

POURING THE FOOTING

1. Oil the forms with clean motor oil or a concrete release agent. Mix and pour the QUIKRETE® Concrete, working from one end of the form to the other. Fill all voids and work out the air pockets by working the end of a rod in and out of the concrete.

Concrete Walls

The clean, smooth lines of a poured concrete wall adapt to any landscape or setting. Easily formed in curves, straight lines, or irregular shapes, walls of concrete are strong and durable with most applications requiring no more than 8" widths.

Concrete walls are widely used as foundations for many types of structures.

Concrete walls can also be used in garden or patio areas as decorative screens, borders, planter walls, tree wells, or retaining walls to control erosion or landscape an area.

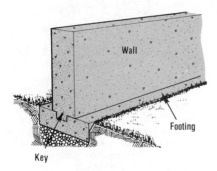

Wall

Footing

Key

Tools and Materials

QUIKRETE® Concrete Mix
QUIKRETE® Sand Mix
QUIKRETE® Concrete Bonding
 Adhesive
Power mixer, square-faced shovel, wheelbarrow, tamper, internal vibrator, screed, level, hand float, drill, hammer, and saw
Reinforcing rebar, forming lumber, stakes, and #8 or #9 steel tie wire

BUILDING THE FORMS

The most important step in constructing a strong, attractive wall is building strong, accurate forms. Wall forms must be strong enough to withstand the great pressure exerted by the wet concrete; any failure in the forms will be disastrous. Keep in mind that building and aligning the forms for a poured concrete wall usually takes much longer than pouring and finishing the concrete.

A straight wall form is constructed of 1/2", 3/4", or 1" plywood sheathing, studs, spacers, ties, and (for larger, heavier walls) wales. Sheathing forms the mold, while studs back up and support the sheathing. Spacers set and maintain spacing and support the form prior to the pour. Wire ties snug the form and resist the pressure of the wet concrete. Wales align the form and brace the studs in forms more than 4' to 5' high. Two horizontal wales are sufficient for most forms, but they should not be spaced greater than 30" on center.

For lower, lighter walls, it is possible to cast the wall at the same time you cast the footer. Larger walls always require separate pours for the footer and wall, with the wall keyed to the footer as shown in the illustration.

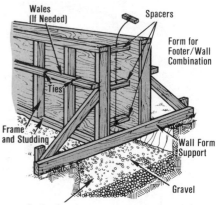

Wales (If Needed)

Spacers

Form for Footer/Wall Combination

Ties

Frame and Studding

Wall Form Support

Gravel

Footing Trench

To construct the forms:

1. Build the form in sections, using 2 × 4s laid on edge to construct frames that measure the height of the wall and no more than 8' in length. Nail 2 × 4 studs into each frame, spacing them on 16" centers.

2. Nail plywood sheathing to the frames. If needed, mark off the position of the wales and toenail them to the studs.

3. To install wire ties, drill 1/8" holes on either side of the wales or studs. Tilt two sections upright, face to face, spacing them at the desired wall thickness. Run a piece of wire through opposite holes in the form and around wales or studs. Twist the ends together to form a loop. Insert a properly sized spacer near the tie, and tighten down the tie by using a stick to twist the tie snug as shown. Remember to

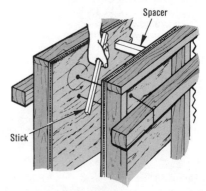

Spacer

Stick

attach pull wires around spacers so they can be removed as the pour is made.

4. Add on additional sections by nailing frames together through adjacent studding. The running length of the form should be slightly longer than the finished wall so that a stop board can be installed as shown.

5. Center the completed form over the footer, making certain it is plumb. Stake, brace, and nail the form firmly in place.

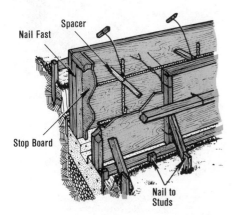

Nail Fast
Spacer
Stop Board
Nail to Studs

POURING THE WALL

1. With the form properly mounted on the cured concrete footer, tie the wall rebar into the existing footer rebar. Coat the insides of the forms with clean oil or release agent.

2. Prepare the QUIKRETE® Concrete Mix to be used for the wall. Avoid using too much water and creating a soupy consistency—aggregates will settle toward the bottom and a weak wall will result.

3. Pour the wall in horizontal layers of not more than 20", beginning at the ends and moving toward the center. Use a ramp to wheel the concrete into position and a splashboard to direct the pour and control spillage. Remove the spacers as you go.

4. Work the concrete against the sides of the form and around the reinforcement as each layer is poured. Use an internal vibrator or strike the sides of the form with a hammer or mallet. Pour layers as soon after the previous one as possible to avoid cold (non-bonded) joints, which cause leaks. For delays of more than 20 minutes be-

tween pours, lay a 1/2" to 1" layer of QUIKRETE® Sand Mix and Concrete Acrylic Fortifier on the previous pour to seal the joint; for delays longer than an hour, coat the surface of the previous pour with QUIKRETE® Concrete Bonding Adhesive before pouring the next layer.

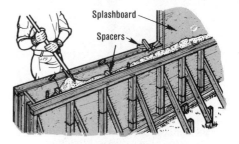

Splashboard
Spacers

5. Strike off the concrete flush with the top of the form. Float and trowel it to the desired finish. Insert anchor bolts for mud sills and wooden caps once the concrete has set sufficiently to hold them.

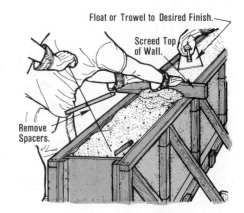

Float or Trowel to Desired Finish.
Screed Top of Wall.
Remove Spacers.

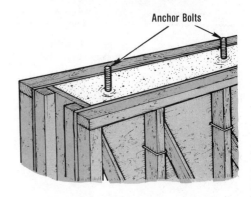

Anchor Bolts

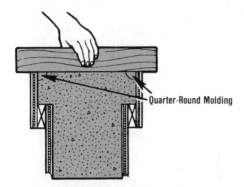

Quarter-Round Molding

6. Remove the forms after the concrete has cured for at least 3 to 4 days. The wire ties will eventually rust and stain the concrete if left in, so cut them out beneath the surface of the concrete. Patch the holes after wetting them down; apply QUIKRETE® Sand Mix or Vinyl Concrete Patcher flush with the surrounding surface.

7. Depending on the amount of concrete to be poured and the people available to do the job, it might be necessary to construct the wall in sections by using a movable stop board. Drill holes through the stop board so that it can be moved along the wall without cutting the rebar.

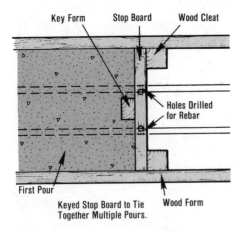

Key Form Stop Board Wood Cleat

Holes Drilled for Rebar

First Pour

Keyed Stop Board to Tie
Together Multiple Pours. Wood Form

8. As each section is poured, allow it to set (12 to 24 hours) before removing the stop board. Before pouring the new section, coat the exposed end with QUIKRETE® Concrete Bonding Adhesive to avoid leaks caused by the cold joint.

For Best Results

Pour long walls in stages using a movable stop board to control the length of the pour. Because rebar must run continuously, drill holes in the stop board to avoid unnecessary cutting of reinforcement.

For curved walls cut partial saw kerfs through the sheathing and bend it to shape.

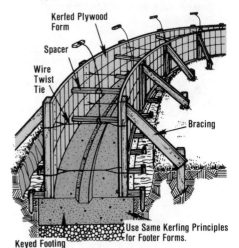

Kerfed Plywood Form

Spacer

Wire Twist Tie

Bracing

Use Same Kerfing Principles for Footer Forms.

Keyed Footing

Forms for Curved Walls

Concrete Retaining Walls

Retaining walls are used to prevent soil erosion of sharply sloping lawns. The principles of solid form construction must be used.

PLANNING THE WALL

Determine the height of the wall. To assure stability, the angle of a sloping lawn should never be greater than 45°, and the gentler the slope, the better. The higher the wall, the gentler the slope will be.

Retaining Wall Construction Data

Exposed Wall Height (A)	Top Thickness (B)	Distance from Ground to Base (C)	Distance from Top to Base (D)	Base Depth (E)	Base Width (F)	Outside Base Extension (G)	Inside Base Extension (H)
12"	6"	4"	16"	14"	6"	3"	3"
18"	6"	6"	24"	18"	6"	3"	3"
24"	7"	8"	32"	24"	8"	4"	4"
30"	7"	10"	40"	28"	10"	4"	4"
36"	8"	12"	48"	36"	12"	6"	6"
42"	8"	14"	56"	40"	12"	6"	6"
48"	9"	16"	64"	44"	12"	6"	6"

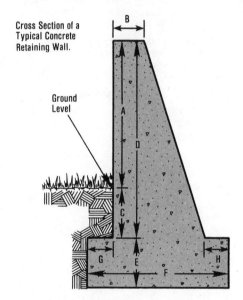

Cross Section of a Typical Concrete Retaining Wall.

the wall, and by building weep holes into the wall. Make weep holes by inserting short lengths of 2" plastic pipe or 3" drain tile in the forms when they are built. The first row should be 2" to 4" above ground level. If the wall is higher than 4', place a second row of weep holes 3' above the first.

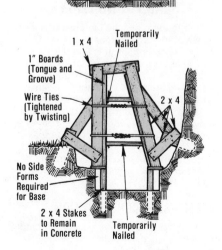

The dimensions of the retaining wall will vary according to the wall height, as shown in the following table. The design shown here does not require steel reinforcement since the width of the base and the weight of the wall provide adequate support.

Good drainage is essential. Drainage is provided by filling coarse gravel behind

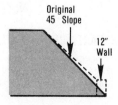

Details of the retaining wall form are shown here. As you can see, footer and wall are cast in one step. If the soil is sufficiently firm, use an earth form for the footer portion.

POURING THE WALL

Follow the mixing and pouring procedure recommended earlier (refer to page 11). Because of the pressure created by the sloping aggregate, cure the concrete for at least 7 days before removing the forms (refer to page 14). Once the forms are removed, tamp crushed stone fill into the space behind the wall. Fill the top foot or so with topsoil, providing a gutter depression along the wall for better drainage.

Concrete Foundations

The three most common foundation designs are poured wall foundations, slab foundations, and pier or pillar foundations. The steps involved in constructing a poured wall foundation are illustrated on pages 11 through 14.

SLAB FOUNDATIONS

Slab foundations are simple and inexpensive, and they eliminate the need for major excavation, footings, and foundation walls. Three variations of slab foundation construction are used: desert, wet/warm area, and cold area. For any type of slab foundation, stake out the area with batter boards (see page 2) and remove the top layer of sod and soil. The tools and materials are similar to those used to pour typical concrete slabs (see page 3). The only exception is the rigid board insulation required for cold area construction.

DESERT SLAB CONSTRUCTION

This type of foundation is constructed the same way as any slab, such as sidewalks or patios, except that a shallow

footing is poured with it. This slab rests directly on the ground.

1. Remove the topsoil and dig the trench as shown.

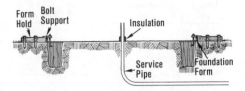

2. Install and insulate any service pipes needed for water, sewer, etc.

3. Construct the forms; stake and nail them firmly in position. Note how anchor bolts can be temporarily positioned for the placing of concrete.

4. Mix and place the concrete in the footer and slab forms in one continuous operation.

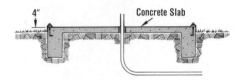

5. Screed, float, and trowel the concrete as if it were a sidewalk or patio (see page 5).

6. When constructing thicker slabs, use 4" of gravel base to save on the amount of concrete used. For larger slabs use a length of 4" × 4" lumber as a temporary screed guide.

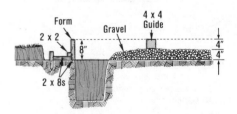

7. Cure the concrete for 3 to 4 days. For information on curing, refer to page 153.

WET/WARM AREA CONSTRUCTION

This type of slab is used in wet/warm areas that are free of freezing problems. The footer and slab sections are poured in two steps, and a moisture barrier is installed.

1. Construct and install two separate forms as shown. Use short lengths of board to hold the inner form in position. Fill the inner form with an 8" gravel base and install a moisture barrier, such as 6-mil plastic sheathing, over the gravel.

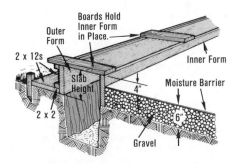

2. Place the concrete in the footer trench 4" short of the top of the form. Allow the concrete time to set up and retain its shape (1 to 2 days).

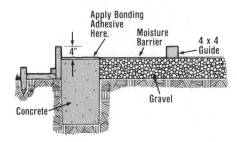

3. Remove the inner form. Apply a coat of QUIKRETE® Concrete Adhesive to the exposed footer surface.

4. Pour, screed, and finish the balance of the slab form, removing the temporary screed guides as you proceed.

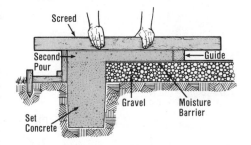

5. Cure the concrete for 3 to 4 days. For information on curing, refer to page 153.

COLD AREA CONSTRUCTION

The footer section of this slab must extend below the frost line, and the slab itself must be insulated with rigid board insulation.

1. Dig a 2'-wide footer trench to a depth several inches below the frost line. In firm soil, one side of the trench can act as a form. Construct and install the outer and inner form walls as shown.

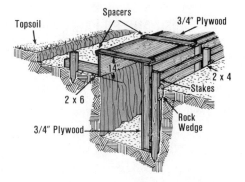

2. Pour the concrete to the top of the form, vibrate out air pockets, screed level, and install anchor bolts.

3. Remove the form and install 4" rigid insulation board on the inner side of the concrete foundation. Use soil to hold the insulation in place.

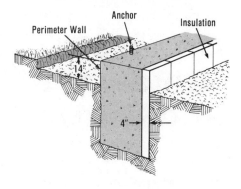

4. Lay down a 6" gravel base, cover with a moisture barrier, and lay rigid board insulation on top of the moisture barrier as shown.

5. Place a 4"-thick layer of concrete over the insulation board, screeding and finishing as before.

6. Cure the concrete for 3 to 4 days. For information on curing, refer to page 153.

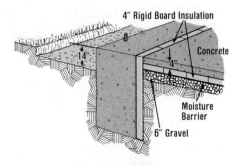

PIER AND PILLAR FOUNDATIONS

A pier or pillar foundation consists of individual footers on which the piers or pillars are placed. These simple foundations are commonly used for small structures with a crawl space design. Anchor bolts or plates are set in the pier so that wood or metal pillars can be erected.

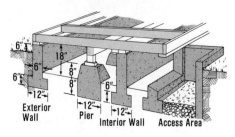

Concrete Driveways and Curbs

Concrete driveways are constructed in the same manner as slabs, with certain key differences in design. Driveways for single-car garages are normally 10' to 14' wide; they must be at least 14' wide if the driveway curves. For two-car garages, the driveway is usually about 24' wide. A good rule of thumb to follow is this: A driveway should be 3' wider than the widest vehicle it will serve.

An alternative to the basic slab driveway is the strip driveway. It has one strip of concrete under each wheel, approximately 3' to 4' wide and 5' center to center, with space between the strips. One caution with this type of driveway, however, is that it shifts more easily with changes in ground conditions than the slab type, and thus requires some type of reinforcement.

Driveway thickness depends solely on the weight of the vehicles that will be using it. If it will serve only passenger cars, 4" is sufficient. If, on the other hand, trucks and other heavy vehicles will be using the driveway, a thickness of 5" or 6" is recommended.

DRIVEWAY GRADE

Driveway grade must be carefully planned if the garage is located above or below street level. A 14% grade (1-3/4" vertical rise for each running foot) is the recommended maximum, and it should be done gradually to avoid scraping the bumper or underside of the vehicles. For drainage purposes, a driveway should always be sloped slightly toward the street; 1/4" per running foot is sufficient. A crown or cross slope can be used for this purpose.

When constructing a driveway after the street, curbs, and public walks are in place, consult your local building codes; the part of the driveway between the street and the sidewalk is usually controlled by the local municipality. If the driveway is built before the public walk, it must meet the proposed sidewalk grade and then drop to meet the top of the curb or gutter.

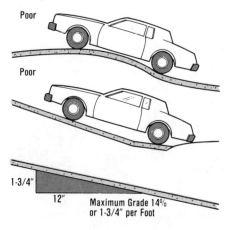

ADDING A CURB

When adding a curb to the end of a driveway, drill two 1/2"-diameter holes into the driveway. These holes should be 3″ deep and approximately 2′ apart. Insert a 6″ steel reinforcing rod in each hole. To construct the forms, stake a 2 × 8 flat against the edge of the driveway; the inside forms cannot be staked, so nail two short 2 × 4s perpendicular to the form, extending in toward the center of the driveway. Use bricks to weigh down the 2 × 4 supports. After pouring the concrete, round the inside edge of the curb with a trowel. This curb will be 6″ wide and extend 4″ above the driveway.

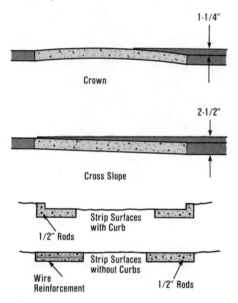

below the threshold of the door. To assure proper drainage, the steps should pitch forward with a slope of approximately 1/4″ per foot.

The height of the riser and depth of the tread are important factors for achieving maximum safety and convenience. Use the following riser/tread proportion chart when building steps.

When Riser Is:	Tread Should Be:
4″ to 4-1/2″	18″ to 19″
5″ to 5-1/2″	16″ to 17″
6″ to 6-1/2″	14″ to 15″
7″ to 7-1/2″	10″ to 11″

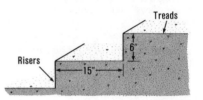

It should be noted that riser and tread size ultimately depends on step use. For a stepped ramp walkway on a long slope, the riser height should be limited to 6″ and the slope between 1/8″ per foot and 1/4″ per foot. In general, wide treads are compatible with a short rise because it allows for a more natural walking stride. Risers and treads must be uniform in any given flight of stairs.

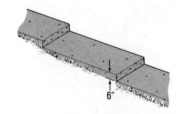

Concrete Steps and Ramps

Steps constructed from QUIKRETE® Concrete Mix are attractive and durable, and can provide good traction in wet weather. For homes, they are usually built 48″ wide, or at least as wide as the door and walk they serve. A landing should be used to divide flights of steps more than 5′ high. It is recommended that landings be no less than 3′ deep, with the top landing no more than 7-1/2″

Tools and Materials

QUIKRETE® Concrete Mix
Sand or gravel (for fill), oil or release agent, 5-ply plywood (for side forms), 2 × 4 and 2 × 8 lumber (for forms and stakes), and double-headed nails
Shovel, rake, wheelbarrow, mixing box or power mixer (depending on size of job), saw, hammer, tape measure, string, level, finishing trowel, wood float, edger, and darby

PREPARING THE BASE

Level the area to be covered by the steps. Clear it of dirt and stones, as well as grass and other organic material. Dig to a depth of 6". Use sand or gravel to bring the site to uniform grade, then compact it by dampening and tamping it down. The base should be solid, uniform, and free of foreign matter. Then, go on to build the forms.

BUILDING THE FORMS

1. Use 1/2" sheets of 5-ply plywood or 2" lumber to build the side forms. Cut the forms according to the planned dimensions of the steps, always allow- ing extra depth for fill below the ground level (see dotted line in illustration).

2. Brace firmly in place with 2 × 4 stakes and diagonal braces running from the top edge of the sides to stakes set firmly in the ground.

3. Use a level to keep the forms perfectly vertical. If the steps are being built against a house or other foundation, be sure to apply a 1/2" mastic expan- sion joint.

4. Coat the inside surfaces of the forms with oil or release agent to make re- moval easier.

5. For variations on building forms, see the illustrations.

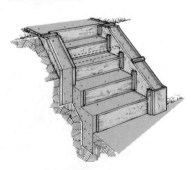

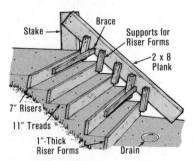

Stake — Brace
Supports for
Riser Forms
2 x 8
Plank
7" Risers
11" Treads
1"-Thick
Riser Forms   Drain

POURING THE CONCRETE AND FINISHING THE SURFACE

1. Fill in any low areas in the forms with gravel, broken brick, or chunks of concrete block; this will also reduce the amount of concrete mix needed. Work the mix in and around all rubble thoroughly. Make sure the rubble is placed back from the form sides so it will not break through the concrete surface.

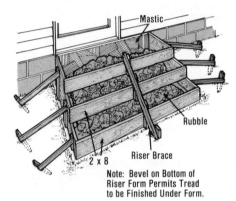

Mastic
Rubble
Riser Brace
2 x 8
Note: Bevel on Bottom of
Riser Form Permits Tread
to be Finished Under Form.

2. It is important to mix the entire project at one time. Overfill the forms slightly, then work the concrete in and out with a shovel to compact the mix and eliminate air pockets.

3. Once the mix has been poured and compacted, screed the surface immediately.

4. Use a float or darby to level any re- maining ridges and fill any voids in the concrete.

5. Once the surface has turned dull, use an edging tool with a 1/2" radius to round the edges.

6. Use a trowel to give the concrete a fi- nal smoothing. Keep the trowel pressed flat against the surface. Sweep it back and forth in an arc, with each pass overlapping half of the pre- vious lap. To produce a textured, non- skid surface, use a wood float for the final troweling.

CURING THE CONCRETE

To help the hardening process, keep the concrete damp for 3 to 4 days after it has been poured. When it has fully cured, remove the side forms. Keep in mind that proper curing of all concrete mixes is essential in order for maximum strength to be achieved.

RAMPS

Ramps can be used in the event of a slight change in elevation; they also come in handy as paths for wheelbarrows, lawn mowers, and other equipment. The only addition to the materials list is 1/2" plywood. Use the plywood for the forms and be sure to stake them securely. Starting at the bottom, pour partially stiff QUIKRETE® Concrete Mix into the forms. Use a trowel to fill in the form, smoothing the surface as you go. Be sure to use partially stiff concrete; if it is too runny, it will not fill the forms completely.

Setting Posts

Tools and Materials

QUIKRETE® Concrete Mix
Gravel or crushed stone
Plumb line or level
Long-handled spade
Wood preservative and/or rust inhibitor
Wood braces and nails (if needed)

QUIKRETE® Concrete Mix makes a solid base for firmly setting wood or metal posts.

1. The diameter of the posthole should be 3 times the post diameter. Hole depth should be 1/3 overall post length. When the post is to be used for structural support, such as for decking, the hole must extend several inches below the frost line. Undercutting the base of the hole with a spade increases support strength. Tamp the sides and bottom of the hole until firm. Do not use forms.

2. Place a 6" gravel base in the hole.

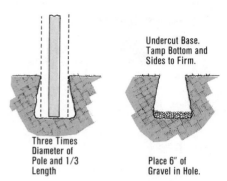

Undercut Base. Tamp Bottom and Sides to Firm.

Three Times Diameter of Pole and 1/3 Length

Place 6" of Gravel in Hole.

3. Add clean water to QUIKRETE® Concrete Mix, mixing to a plastic-like consistency. Coat the gravel base with concrete, working it into the gravel with a spade.

4. Position the post on the gravel, checking to see that the post is level and plumb.

5. Fill the remaining hole with QUIKRETE® Concrete Mix. Recheck plumb and position.

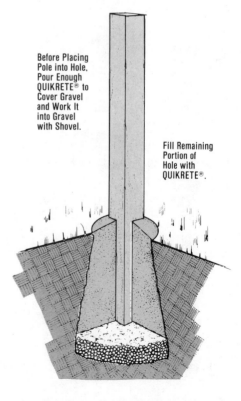

Before Placing Pole into Hole, Pour Enough QUIKRETE® to Cover Gravel and Work It into Gravel with Shovel.

Fill Remaining Portion of Hole with QUIKRETE®.

6. Moist-cure the concrete by keeping it damp for 5 to 7 days before placing stress on the post.

Brace posts in correct position during pouring and setting.

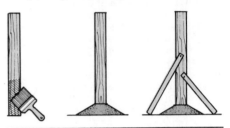

For Best Results

Use pressure-treated wood or apply creosote equivalent to prevent below-ground rot. Coat metal posts with rust inhibitor.

Dig larger, dish-shaped holes for posts set in loose or sandy soil.

Slope concrete away from posts to direct water away from post foundations.

Gallery of Post Setting Projects

Stable wooden and metal posts and support pieces set in QUIKRETE® Concrete Mix form the backbone of dozens of successful, useful, and enjoyable home projects.

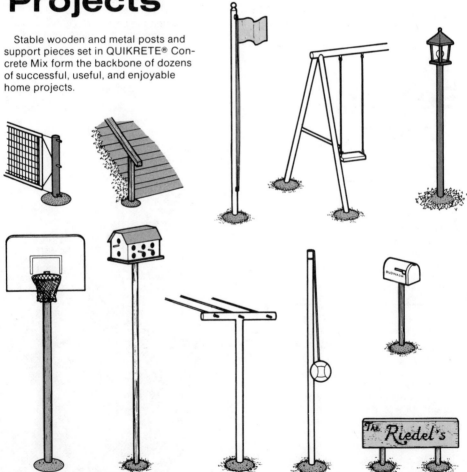

Fence and Trellis Designs

Perhaps the most popular home project involving the setting of posts is fence building. All fences, from simple two-rail designs to more elaborate split-rail and picket designs, need solid support.

Tools and Materials

Fence posts are available in 4" × 4", 6" × 6", or 8" × 8" sizes cut to any desired length. Rails are usually 2" × 4" lumber cut to 6', 8', or 10' lengths. Fence pickets, capping rails, and other decorative pieces are readily available at any reputable lumberyard.

In addition to the tools outlined under *Setting Posts,* you'll need the following: auger or clamshell digger, measuring tape, string, stakes, saw, hammer, nails, and gate hardware.

PLANNING

1. Before beginning work, check with local authorities to see if there are any ordinances, regulations, or zoning laws concerning the height, location, and materials for fences in your locality. Your property deed may also contain restrictions concerning the construction of fences.

2. Be absolutely certain of your property lines; have the area surveyed if necessary. If you mistakenly build a fence on a neighbor's property, the fence is his, and he has the right to remove it, paint it, etc.

PLOTTING THE FENCE

1. Plot the line of the fence to avoid major visible obstacles such as trees and boulders, and also make sure you are away from all underground utilities before digging postholes. In most cases, a call to your phone, gas, cable, and/or electric company will prompt a free visit to your property to make any necessary alterations.

2. Measure the fence's overall length, allowing space for one or more gates if desired. Divide this length into equal intervals of 6', 8', or 10'. In this way standard precut lumber can be used for the crossrails, minimizing cutting waste. If one section is smaller, consider using it as a gate location.

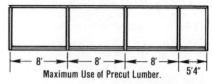

Maximum Use of Precut Lumber.

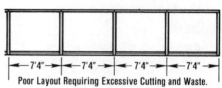

Poor Layout Requiring Excessive Cutting and Waste.

3. To find the exact post locations, mark both end points of the fence with wooden stakes and run a line between them. Locate positions for all posts between the end posts by measuring intervals with a tape, or by laying out the precut rails in line along the ground.

SETTING POSTS

1. Dig the postholes vertically straight and in the correct locations, using a hand or power auger if the soil is free of stones, or a clamshell-type digger if the soil is rocky.

2. Set the first end post on its gravel base, and pour a collar of QUIKRETE® Concrete Mix. Use a carpenter's level

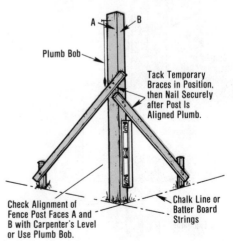

Plumb Bob

Tack Temporary Braces in Position, then Nail Securely after Post Is Aligned Plumb.

Check Alignment of Fence Post Faces A and B with Carpenter's Level or Use Plumb Bob.

Chalk Line or Batter Board Strings

and plumb bob to align the post 90°
vertically.

3. Set the second end post firmly on its
gravel base, but do not immediately
pour concrete in its hole. Run a string
between the tops of these two posts,
and then position the interval posts,
carefully aligning and bracing them
vertically. Make sure the posts are
correctly spaced and that the tops of
all posts are level with one another.

4. Mix and pour collars of QUIKRETE®
Concrete Mix for all remaining posts.
Double-check for plumbness. Allow
the concrete to cure 3 to 4 days before adding the rails and facing.

FINISHING

1. Attach the top rail or stringer first.
This rail is usually placed flat on top
of posts to keep the fence in
alignment.

2. Various types of butt, lap, dado, and
mortise-and-tenon joints can be used
to fasten rails to posts.

Joints for Post and Rail Construction

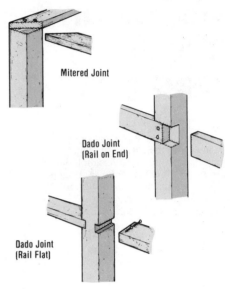

Mitered Joint

Dado Joint
(Rail on End)

Dado Joint
(Rail Flat)

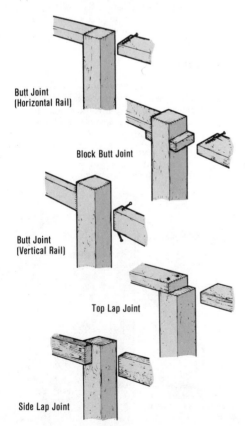

Butt Joint
(Horizontal Rail)

Block Butt Joint

Butt Joint
(Vertical Rail)

Top Lap Joint

Side Lap Joint

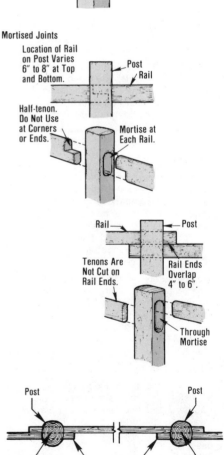

Mortised Joints

Location of Rail
on Post Varies
6" to 8" at Top
and Bottom.

Post

Rail

Half-tenon.
Do Not Use
at Corners
or Ends.

Mortise at
Each Rail.

Rail

Post

Tenons Are
Not Cut on
Rail Ends.

Rail Ends
Overlap
4" to 6".

Through
Mortise

Post

Post

Mortise

Rail

Rail

Mortise

Simple Method for Uniform
Spacing of Pickets for Fences.

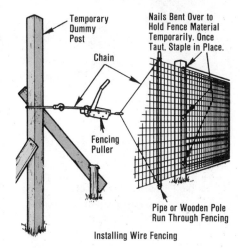

Installing Wire Fencing

Temporary
Dummy
Post

Chain

Fencing
Puller

Nails Bent Over to
Hold Fence Material
Temporarily. Once
Taut, Staple in Place.

Pipe or Wooden Pole
Run Through Fencing

3. With the top rail in place, measure down the post to position bottom and middle rails. Before attaching rails to posts, apply paint or wood preservative to cut ends of the lumber.

4. Facing can be done with wood patterns, pickets, wire screen, or solid panels.

For Best Results

If the ground is not level, make sure that you account for differences so that the fence is even. The ground should be built up and cut back so as not to give a choppy appearance.

On severely sloping ground, be sure to erect posts plumb to one another and then tilt the rails as needed to follow the slope. Tilting the rails

changes the lengths required to span posts, so make sure you don't come up short when using standard lengths of lumber.

Wrong

Right

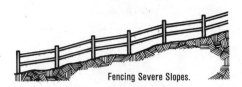

Fencing Slightly Uneven Terrain.

Fencing Severe Slopes.

TRELLISES

A trellis to support perennial vines or roses can make a handsome addition to any garden, patio, or landscaped area. Trellises can stand alone, against a building or entranceway, or as part of a fence/windbreak construction.

Although young vines start out quite slender and fragile, by the end of the growing season they can be extremely heavy and full. Use posts of the dimensions used in fence construction, and attach sturdy rail and crosspieces.

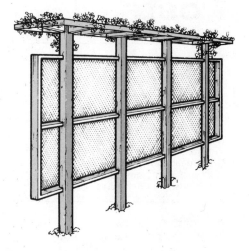

For Best Results

Treat the trellis with nontoxic wood preservative (never creosote).

Apply three coats of quality outdoor paint. Consider matching the color of your house or that of the vine blossoms.

Cast Posts

Tools and Materials

QUIKRETE® Sand Mix or QUIKWALL® Surface Bonding Cement
1/4" plywood or boards for forms, decorative molding strips, and nails
Oil or concrete release agent
Square trowel or straightedge
1/2" threaded rod
1/2" steel reinforcing rod (if needed)
Conduit and hardware (as needed)

QUIKRETE® Sand Mix and QUIKWALL® Surface Bonding Cement can be cast into easy-to-make forms to create a variety of post designs with comparatively small cross sections. Cast posts can have their own bases or be set in concrete.

1. Make wooden forms carefully, using a minimum of parts so stripping will be easy. Coat all concrete-contact surfaces with oil or concrete release agent.

Wooden Forms

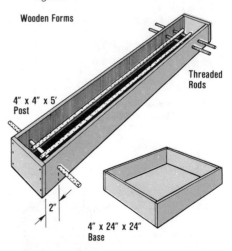

Threaded Rods

4" x 4" x 5' Post

2"

4" x 24" x 24" Base

2. Pour freshly mixed QUIKRETE® Concrete Mix or QUIKWALL® Surface Bonding Cement into the forms, leveling with a square trowel or straightedge. Fill the form completely.

3. Let stand for at least 48 hours before removing the forms. Moist-cure for 3 to 4 days as described earlier.

For Best Results

Use wood moldings to create more stylish posts.

Install 1/2" reinforcement rods when making solid posts.

Install conduit or pipe in posts that will contain electrical cables.

Install any brackets, bolts, studs, hinges, light fixtures, hangers, etc., before the concrete has set.

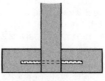

Base

Portable Posts

Portable posts have a number of uses, including clothesline posts, tetherball posts, and supports for badminton or volleyball nets. They are easily made with a heavy-gauge steel pole, a pipe sleeve (with an inside diameter equal to the outside diameter of the pole), a 5-gallon drum, and a base made from QUIKRETE® Concrete Mix.

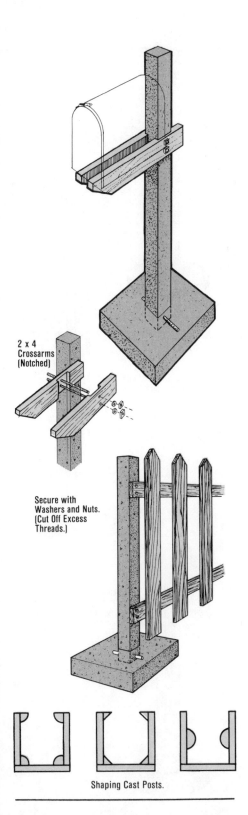

2 x 4
Crossarms
(Notched)

Secure with
Washers and Nuts.
(Cut Off Excess
Threads.)

Shaping Cast Posts.

Tools and Materials

QUIKRETE® Concrete Mix
Heavy-gauge steel pole, 5-gallon
  drum, and pipe sleeve
Square-faced shovel, trowel, tamper,
  tire, and plywood sheet (optional)

---

1. Sink a 5-gallon drum into the ground, so that its top surface is just below grade. Be sure that the base it rests on is firm and level. (If a 5-gallon drum is not available, you can set the pole and sleeve directly into a concrete-filled hole in the ground.)

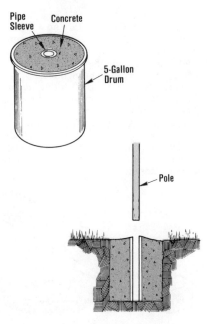

Pipe
Sleeve

Concrete

5-Gallon
Drum

Pole

2. Position the pipe sleeve and pole in the center of the drum, then fill the drum with QUIKRETE® Concrete Mix. Make sure that the pole is plumb.

Another approach utilizes a discarded automobile tire as a permanent, above-grade form. This design supplies ample rigidity, and can be easily moved by tilting the post and rolling it about on the tire.

1. Place the tire on firm, level ground or on a sheet of plywood.

2. Center the post or sleeve and pour QUIKRETE® Concrete Mix around it.

3. Tamp enough concrete to fill the tire completely. Use enough QUIKRETE® Concrete Mix to slope the top surface so that it drains water.

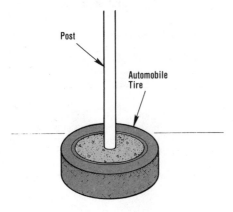

Post

Automobile Tire

A wooden or QUIKWALL® post mounted on a QUIKWALL® base is a design capable of numerous uses as temporary fencing, including party lawn dividers, crowd-control barricades, hurdles, horse jumps, cattle pens, and so on. QUIKWALL® weighs as much as concrete, but its fiber reinforcing makes it less brittle as well as stronger and more malleable than concrete, which allows it to be cast in smaller dimensions. A bolt set in the base allows disassembly for easy storage.

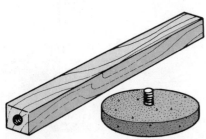

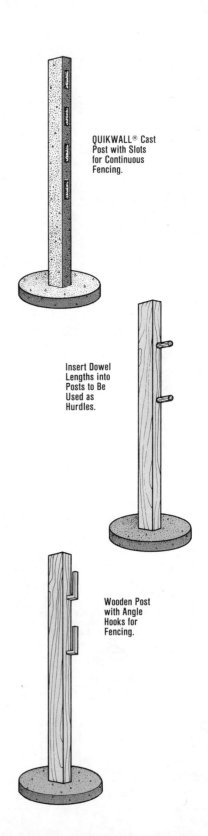

QUIKWALL® Cast Post with Slots for Continuous Fencing.

Insert Dowel Lengths into Posts to Be Used as Hurdles.

Wooden Post with Angle Hooks for Fencing.

Cast Concrete Projects

QUIKRETE® Sand Mix and QUIK-WALL® Surface Bonding Cement are flexible enough to be used in a variety of cast projects. For even greater sculptur-ability with thin projects such as plaques, QUIKRETE® Quick-Setting Cement is ideal. Its fast setting time allows it to be removed from the form and either carved with a utility knife or worked in some other fashion.

While 2 × 4s are most commonly used to build forms for concrete slabs and walls, cast projects use a wide range of form materials. Tin cans, buckets, card-board boxes, mailing tubes, and automo-bile tires can be used to create useful in-door and outdoor accessories. You can also create interesting effects depending on the specific form material you use. For example, unplaned or re-sawed lumber leaves a wood grain effect on the concrete, while lining the form with heavy kraft paper or plastic produces a smooth finish.

For Best Results

Use double-headed nails when build-ing temporary wood forms. Drive the nails to the first head only, leaving the second head exposed for easy removal.

When working with any type of wood form, apply a thin coating of engine

oil to the form before pouring the concrete. This will allow the concrete to set more easily, while reducing the chance of damaging the concrete when it is removed from the form.

Always give a cast project plenty of time to cure before attempting to re-move it.

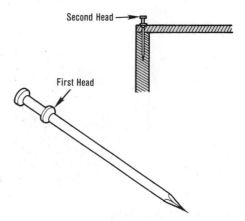

When removing a cast project from a form, do so very carefully. Place it in the shade on a platform that allows for air space underneath the project. Cover with burlap or a thick layer of newspaper and keep this covering wet for at least one week.

As an added touch, cast projects can be painted, stained, or coated with plastic aluminum or steel for a metal-lic effect.

BOOKENDS

Here's a project that's great for the scout in your family or anyone else— sturdy concrete bookends.

Tools and Materials

QUIKRETE® Sand Mix, QUIKWALL® Surface Bonding Cement, or QUIK-RETE® Quick-Setting Cement Coffee tin, felt, wood divider, and trowel

1. Place a tight-fitting wood divider into a 2- or 3-lb. coffee tin as shown.

2. Pour the QUIKRETE® Sand Mix, QUIKWALL® Surface Bonding Ce-ment, or QUIKRETE® Quick-Setting

Cement into the tin, filling it completely.

3. Use a trowel to smooth the surface of the concrete.

4. When the concrete has cured completely, cut away the tin. The bookends can be easily carved with a knife if you want to add any decorative features. Finally, glue a piece of felt to the bottom of each bookend to avoid scratching furniture.

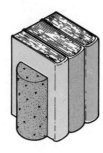

ANCHORS

An anchor was never this easy to make; just follow these step-by-step directions.

Tools and Materials

QUIKRETE® Sand Mix or QUIK-WALL® Surface Bonding Cement Bucket or can, anchor bolt, and trowel

1. Start this project with an old bucket, a large can, or a similar container.

2. Pour QUIKRETE® Sand Mix or QUIKWALL® Surface Bonding Cement into the container, filling it completely. After about 20 to 30 minutes, place an anchor bolt in the container as shown. Trowel the surface smooth.

3. Do not attempt to use the anchor until the concrete has cured completely. If

additional weight is needed, make several anchors and join them with chain.

WHEEL CHOCKS

This project is perfect for the "Saturday mechanic"—wheel chocks connected by clothesline for easy transporting.

Tools and Materials

QUIKRETE® Sand Mix or QUIK-WALL® Surface Bonding Cement Cardboard boxes, utility knife, masking tape, clothesline, anchor bolts, and trowel

1. Start with two cardboard boxes approximately 8″ × 12″ × 6″. Remove one of the small sides from each box. Next, use a utility knife to remove half of each rectangular side, cutting diagonally as shown. The forms for the wheel chocks are now complete.

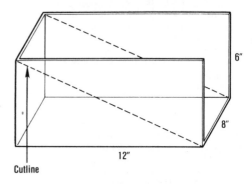

Cutline

2. Use masking tape to fortify the 6″ side of the forms, then prop up the forms 3″ to 4″ with wood blocks as shown.

3. With the utility knife, puncture a small hole in the center of the 6″ sides. Insert an anchor bolt into the boxes; when the concrete hardens, the bolts

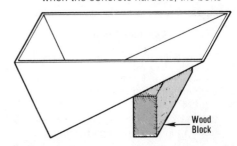

Wood Block

will become firmly set in the wheel chocks.

4. Pour the QUIKRETE® Sand Mix or QUIKWALL® Surface Bonding Cement into the boxes, filling them completely.

5. When the concrete has partially hardened (about 20 to 30 minutes), smooth it with a trowel, then take the forms off the wood blocks.

6. When the concrete has cured completely, rip away the cardboard boxes. As an easy way of carrying both wheel chocks at once, tie each end of a short length of clothesline around the anchor bolts and use the rope as a handle.

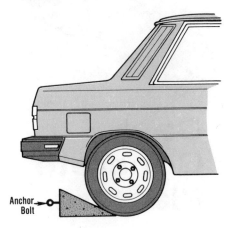

even want to try letters and numbers—you're only as limited as your imagination. Make sure all cuts are beveled slightly toward what will be the inside of the forms.

3. Use strips of 1 × 2 wood as a border around the perimeter of the plywood.

4. Set the entire assembly, plywood side down, on a compact sand bed and apply a thin coating of engine oil. Pour the QUIKRETE® Sand Mix, QUIKWALL® Surface Bonding Cement, or QUIKRETE® Quick-Setting Cement slowly into the form. Be sure that the cutout areas are filled, then smooth the concrete with a trowel so that it is level with the upper edges of the border.

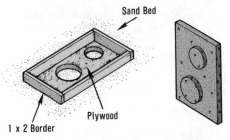

5. Let the concrete cure for at least 48 hours, then turn the form over carefully and remove the plaque. Remember: Oiling the form prior to casting will make removal easier.

6. The plaque is pliable enough to be carved if you wish to add any decorative grooving.

PLAQUES

This raised concrete plaque can be hung on a wall, placed on a table, or combined with other materials to create an unusual conversation piece.

Tools and Materials

QUIKRETE® Sand Mix, QUIKWALL® Surface Bonding Cement, or QUIKRETE® Quick-Setting Cement Plywood, 1 × 2 wood strips, saw (keyhole, saber, or jigsaw), and trowel

1. Cut a sheet of 1/2″ or 3/4″ plywood to the desired size.

2. Use a keyhole saw, saber saw, or jigsaw to cut openings in the plywood. The openings can be simple circles, as in the illustration, or as intricate as plant and animal shapes. You may

DOWNSPOUT SPLASH GUARDS

A concrete downspout splash guard is durable, long-lasting, and easy to build with these step-by-step directions.

Tools and Materials

QUIKRETE® Sand Mix, QUIKWALL® Surface Bonding Cement, or QUIKRETE® Quick-Setting Cement Crushed stone or gravel, 1 × 4 forming lumber, stakes, nails, shovel, and trowel

1. Dig a trench the required length; it should be approximately 12″ wide and 6″ deep.

2. Use 1 × 4 lumber to build the forms. Stake and nail boards firmly in place, then apply a thin coating of engine oil to the form.

3. Pour QUIKRETE® Sand Mix, QUIK-WALL® Surface Bonding Cement, or QUIKRETE® Quick-Setting Cement into the form. Use a trowel to shape the gutter as shown; it should be at least 4″ deep at its deepest point. Allow at least 1 week curing time before using.

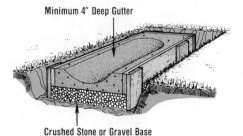

Minimum 4″ Deep Gutter

Crushed Stone or Gravel Base

4. Be certain to always slope the gutter away from the downspout in order to maintain proper drainage.

GARDEN EDGING/CURBING

To accentuate your home's exterior, try this project—garden edging/curbing.

Tools and Materials

QUIKRETE® Sand Mix or QUIK-WALL® Surface Bonding Cement
1 × 2 lumber and trowel

1. Construct a V-shaped form from 1 × 2s; a good workable length is 4′, although this can vary.

2. As shown in the cross section, the form should be approximately 10″ high and at least 4″ wide at its widest point, which will eventually be the base of the edging. Making the base

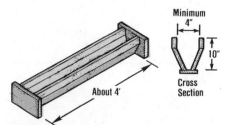

About 4′

Minimum 4″

10″

Cross Section

any narrower will cause the edging/curbing to be too unstable.

3. Apply a thin coating of engine oil to the form. Pour QUIKRETE® Sand Mix or QUIKWALL® Surface Bonding Cement into the form, filling it completely. Trowel the surface smooth, then allow at least 48 hours curing time before removing it from the form.

4. If you want to stake the edging/curbing into the ground, simply cast the project with holes in the center as shown.

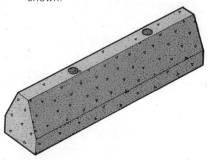

Cast Concrete Planters

In this project, you'll learn to build both a rectangular and a round planter.

RECTANGULAR PLANTER

Tools and Materials

QUIKRETE® Sand Mix, QUIKWALL® Surface Bonding Cement, or QUIKRETE® Quick-Setting Cement
3/4″ plywood, drill, dowel, cardboard box or similar container, tamper, and oil

1. Use 3/4″ plywood to build the forms according to the following dimensions: 10-3/4″ × 14-3/4″ × 3/4″ short sides, 10-3/4″ × 17-3/4″ × 3/4″ long sides, and 17-1/2″ × 17-3/4″ × 1-1/2″ bottom.

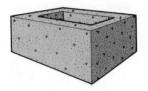

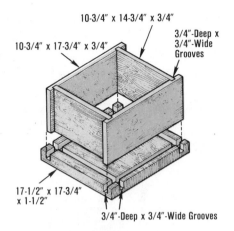

10-3/4″ x 14-3/4″ x 3/4″

10-3/4″ x 17-3/4″ x 3/4″

3/4″-Deep x 3/4″-Wide Grooves

17-1/2″ x 17-3/4″ x 1-1/2″

3/4″-Deep x 3/4″-Wide Grooves

diately after removing them, then set them aside for future use. (They must always be re-oiled before each use.) Allow the concrete to cure 3 to 4 days before using the planter.

8. To add color and durability, consider painting the planter with QUIKRETE® Masonry Coating.

ROUND PLANTER

Tools and Materials

QUIKRETE® Sand Mix, QUIKWALL® Surface Bonding Cement, or QUIKRETE® Quick-Setting Cement Sand, wastebasket or similar container, drill, dowel, inner form, oil, and tamper

2. Assemble the form by means of a groove system as shown in the illustration. Cut the grooves 3/4″ deep × 3/4″ wide; for extra rigidity, the sides and ends can be held together with strong cord.

3. Drill a 1/2″ hole through the center of the bottom, then plug it with an oiled dowel that is long enough to penetrate the casting. The dowel will act as a drain hole for the casting.

4. Prepare the inner form by filling a cardboard box, a large can, or even a wastebasket with sand. For a double-cavity planter, use two containers. Do not put the inner form in place until after the concrete base has been poured.

5. To make removing the form easier, coat the inside with a thin layer of oil.

1. Round planters can be cast in a pile of damp sand; building wood forms is not necessary. Scoop out an approximate-sized hole in the sand, then use a wastebasket, drum, or similar container to complete the cavity.

2. Compact the sand around the container. As you bear down on the container, twist it to make a good impression. When removing the container, twist it as you lift.

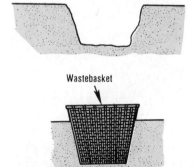

Wastebasket

6. To cast the planter, pour the base layer of concrete, add the inner form, then fill in around it. Use a tamper to firm the concrete around the form as the pouring progresses.

7. When the concrete has set, remove the form. Clean the form parts imme-

3. Pour some of the mix to form the base, then insert a greased dowel to form the drain hole as shown. Make

sure the dowel is long enough to penetrate the casting.

4. Choose a container for the inner form. It should be similar to the container used to form the cavity, but smaller; a square box or some type of cylinder are good choices as long as they provide adequate wall thickness.

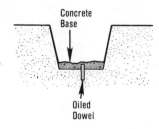

Concrete
Base

Oiled
Dowel

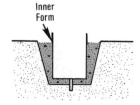

Inner
Form

5. When the inner form is in place, pour the remaining concrete around it. Use a tamper to form the concrete around the form while you pour.

6. Wet-cure the planter in the sand for 3 to 4 days.

7. To add color and durability, consider painting the planter with QUIKRETE® Masonry Coating.

Anchoring Projects

Use QUIKRETE® Anchoring Cement to fasten objects to concrete for quick use. Anchoring cement expands as it cures, and after 24 hours, it has a pull-out strength of 12,500 pounds. Depending on the amount of water used with the mix, the cement will achieve a final set only 15 to 45 minutes after application.

FLOOR MOUNTINGS

Anchoring cement's exceptional strength and quick-setting characteristics are ideal for fastening heavy-duty industrial machinery. But its simple application makes it just as desirable for home use in projects such as anchoring bolts, posts, wrought-iron railing, signs, workshop machines, and door stops.

Tools and Materials

QUIKRETE® Anchoring Cement
Star drill and hammer or 1/2″ electric
  drill with masonry bit
Small brush

ANCHORING

1. Mark the location of the holes for the bolts.

2. Make a hole at least 1″ larger than the diameter of the object to be anchored. For large objects such as metal pipes or fence posts, use a diamond-edge cold chisel and a small sledgehammer to make the hole. The hole must be at least 2″ deep.

3. Brush all dirt, dust, and other loose material from the hole. Dampen the interior of the hole.

4. Insert the object to be anchored and pour the prepared mix into the hole to the surface level. Anchoring cement can also be packed in with a trowel;

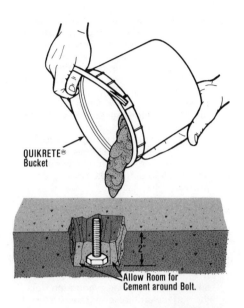

QUIKRETE®
Bucket

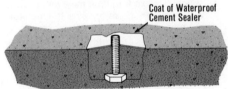

Allow Room for
Cement around Bolt.

Coat of Waterproof
Cement Sealer

when using this method, be sure to completely fill the hole.

5. Hold the object being anchored in place until the mix begins to stiffen. This will depend on the amount of water used to prepare the mix.

6. Wait about 45 minutes before fastening anything to the bolt or post to allow the mix time to achieve a final set.

For Best Results

Use only clean water and containers to prepare the mix.

Apply a coat of waterproof cement sealer to outside projects after the mix obtains a final set.

Apply QUIKRETE® Concrete Bonding Adhesive to holes with smooth interior surfaces before applying QUIKRETE® Anchoring Cement.

Use QUIKRETE® Concrete and Asphalt Cleaner to make certain that any oil or other film that could prevent bonding has been cleaned from the hole.

WALL MOUNTINGS

Anchoring cement is a nonshrink grout that is stronger than concrete. Its quick setup time and great strength make it the ideal choice for a wide range of anchoring projects, including bolts, brackets, hooks, racks, shelves, pulleys, and awning and canopy mounts.

Tools and Materials

QUIKRETE® Anchoring Cement
Star drill and hammer or 1/2″ electric drill with masonry bit
Small brush and trowel

ANCHORING

1. Mark on the concrete the location of the hole(s) for the hook or mounting bolts.

2. Make a hole at least 2″ deep and about 3 times the diameter of the bolt or hook to be inserted.

3. Brush all dirt, dust, and other loose material out of the hole.

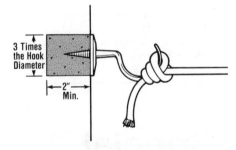

3 Times the Hook Diameter

2″ Min.

4. Dampen the interior of the hole; leave no standing water. Insert the hook or bolt and pack the prepared mix firmly around it to just above surface level. Prepare only as much mix as can be applied in 10 minutes.

5 & 10 CENT STORE

5. Hold the bolt or hook in place until the mix begins to stiffen. (It generally takes only a few minutes. Mix prepared with large amounts of water will take longer.)

6. After all the bolts have set for about 45 minutes, attach any mounting brackets that your project requires. Except for the most unusually heavy objects, mounting can be done after a few hours. Anchoring cement has a compressive strength of 3,000 psi after 2 hours.

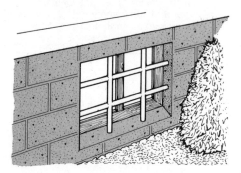

For Best Results

Use only clean containers and water to prepare the mix.

For exterior use, apply a coat of waterproof cement sealer after 45 minutes.

Special Concrete Finishes

There are many alternatives to the standard smooth concrete finish; to select the right one, it is important to make a few practical considerations. For example, will the surface require frequent and thorough cleaning? If so, you should probably stick with a smooth finish, which is much easier to maintain than finishes that are grooved or striated. Also, will the surface be subjected to

freeze/thaw conditions, abrasion, or heavy traffic? If so, avoid splattered finishes, which are more likely to peel and spall. And, if the surface will be subjected to traffic, is good traction a requirement? If so, plan to apply a floated, rough aggregate or an evenly grooved finish because they provide the best footing. Once all the practical considerations have been made, you can make your final decision based on such factors as visual appeal, color scheme, and location. Keep in mind that you can use a combination of finishes in a single project.

When a coarse finish is desired for non-slip footing, floating, edging, and grooving may be the only steps performed. When a denser, smoother finish is required, the surface is troweled once or several times with a stainless steel trowel. Troweling takes place after the surface moisture has evaporated from the surface and the concrete has lost its sheen. This setting time may vary greatly with weather conditions and the moisture content of the mix, from 30 minutes to several hours. Thirty minutes to an hour is average in most cases.

Tools and Materials
(as needed, depending on type of finish desired)

QUIKRETE® Concrete Mix
QUIKRETE® Sand Mix
QUIKRETE® Concrete Bonding Adhesive
QUIKRETE® Surface Bonding Cement
QUIKRETE® Concrete Acrylic Fortifier
QUIKRETE® All-Purpose Sand or Play Sand
Forms or molds, shovel, tamper, screed, darby or bull float, wooden hand float, rectangular trowel, steel trowel, masonry brush, broom, rake, burlap, hose, polyethylene sheeting, joint strips, dividers, oil, decorative stone, aggregate, and dry pigment or concrete stain

---

ROUGH-FLOATED FINISH

Rough concrete provides good traction, so it is particularly suited for pool decks and other areas frequently exposed to water. It is also more durable than smooth concrete. Work the concrete with a wooden hand float; if the surface is very large, use a darby or bull float. Move the float in various patterns until the desired effect is achieved.

SMOOTH FINISH

A smooth finish is practical, easy to clean, and ideal for making decorative inscriptions and impressions. Use a steel trowel, moving it in sweeping arcs; overlap the arcs to make sure the entire slab is smooth.

For very smooth surfaces, additional trowelings are necessary. On the second troweling, hold the leading edge up slightly and press down a bit harder. Repeat the process used in the first troweling. The third troweling should produce an almost glossy finish. Hold the leading edge up further, press down harder, and repeat the troweling process.

First Troweling

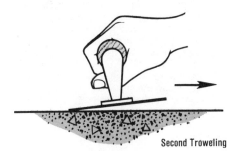

Second Troweling

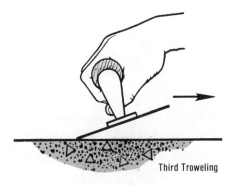

Third Troweling

BROOMED FINISHES

Brooming can achieve a wide range of effects, depending on how soon you apply the broom, whether the bristles are soft or hard, and whether you use it wet or dry. Simply pull the broom across the concrete while it is still soft. A damp, stiff-bristled broom produces a coarse texture, while a dry, soft-bristled broom creates a finer texture. Always pull the broom toward you in parallel, slightly overlapping strokes; never push it back and forth. Use the broom to create curves, waves, even herringbone patterns.

GROOVED AND STAMPED FINISHES

Grooved and stamped finishes are produced by pressing masonry stamping tools and other objects into slightly stiff concrete. A piece of bent pipe works particularly well for making deep, clean grooves, and a jointer can be used to groove the concrete to look like flagstone. You can create a wide range of surface designs, including brick shapes, stone shapes, and tile shapes. For a

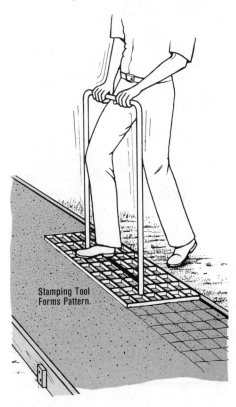

Stamping Tool Forms Pattern.

unique finish, create your own home-made stamp using typical household items such as cookie cutters.

Use a Jointing Tool to Groove the Concrete to Look Like Flagstone.

SPLATTERED FINISH

Splattered finishes are undeniably beautiful and unusual, but they are also less durable than other finishes and are most often used on walks. The most common splattered finish is the travertine effect; this is achieved by first applying QUIKRETE® Concrete Bonding Adhesive to the concrete. When it becomes tacky, splatter a 1/2″ layer of QUIKRETE® Sand Mix onto the surface with a large brush and trowel very lightly over the high spots.

RUBBED AND HAMMERED AGGREGATE FINISHES

A powdery, dusty effect can be produced by applying a thin layer of QUIKRETE® All-Purpose Sand or Play

Sand onto a concrete surface that has partially set. Shake the sand over the entire surface, then rub it in using a piece of clean burlap.

Medium-sized aggregate (including pebbles, small gravel, and seashell fragments) can be hammered into fresh concrete. Use a screed to evenly distribute the force of each blow.

EXPOSED-STONE AND COARSE-AGGREGATE FINISHES

Stones of various shapes and sizes can be individually hand-set or sown like seeds onto a surface of slightly stiff concrete. Coarse aggregate, such as large gravel, may be applied in the same way. Be sure to use clean, damp stones; after the application, press them into the mix (or slightly under the surface) with a heavy screed. Next, use a stiff-bristled broom to remove any excess mortar. Finally, clean the surface with a fine spray of water until there is no noticeable cement film left on the aggregate.

ly, then repeat the procedure with the remaining material. In either case, follow the instructions for the specific coloring agent you are using.

Rip Rap Projects:
Dams, Bulkheads, and Erosion Control Walls

QUIKRETE® Concrete and Sand mixes are packaged in biodegradable paper bags suitable for rip rapping to save time and labor on heavy-duty projects. They are ideal for constructing headwalls for culverts and other erosion control projects, as well as for building dams, beach bulkheads, and waterway walls. They are also especially useful in out-of-the-way locations and eliminate the need for costly construction machinery. A particular advantage in their use is the ability to set in a wide range of conditions, from water immersion to natural moisture alone.

DAMS AND BULKHEADS

A sturdy, long-lasting dam or bulkhead is a relatively quick and simple job with rip rap. The 60-lb. bag is suggested because of its easy handling. When estimating rip rap needs, figure five bags for 7 linear feet and three bags for each vertical foot.

2'

3 Bags per Foot |← 7' (Approximately 5 Bags) →|

Approximately 170 1/2 Cu Ft Bags Are Needed for a 100 Sq Ft Area.

Tools and Materials

QUIKRETE® Concrete or Sand Mix
Steel reinforcing rods (staple or straight)
Sledgehammer and shovel

COLORED FINISHES

One method of coloring concrete is to add mineral pigment to the mix itself. Measure the pigment carefully; it should never exceed 10% of the weight of the mix. When coloring concrete in batches, the proportions must be carefully controlled to achieve uniform results.

A second coloring method involves spreading dry coloring material over the concrete after it has been leveled and floated. Apply about two-thirds of the total amount of coloring material in a first application, finish as you would normal-

CONSTRUCTION

1. Outline the area to be excavated, extending the excavation at least 1' beyond the edge of the planned wall. Remove all grass, roots, and other organic matter. Dig to a depth of 6" and bring the base of this trench to a uniform grade.

2. Lay the first tier of bags for the dam or bulkhead wall by butting the bags together end-to-end. Stack succeeding tiers in an interlocking fashion or bond pattern. Thoroughly sprinkle and tamp each layer of bags. Perforating the bags with a pitchfork or metal rake will speed saturation and initial set.

3. To increase the wall's strength, 3/8" steel rebar staples can be driven into the bags. Alternate the staple direction from bag to bag and tier to tier.

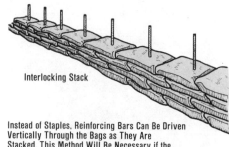

Interlocking Stack

Instead of Staples, Reinforcing Bars Can Be Driven Vertically Through the Bags as They Are Stacked. This Method Will Be Necessary if the Bags Are Stacked Under Water.

For Best Results

The work should be completed with as little interruption as possible to assure integral construction.

Materials should be kept wet for 4 days to assist curing, although natural moisture alone is enough to set.

Walls higher than 10' should be temporarily sway braced with 2 × 4s to facilitate initial set.

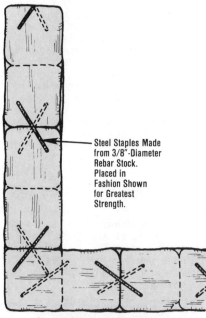

Steel Staples Made from 3/8"-Diameter Rebar Stock. Placed in Fashion Shown for Greatest Strength.

Alternate Directions of Staples from Bag to Bag and Tier to Tier.

Interlocking Dam and Wing Walls

4. As an alternative, drive straight rebar rods down through the bags as shown. This method is needed if the bags are stacked under water.

5. Depending on the height of the dam wall and the capacity of the reservoir, it may be desirable to leave channels for water runoff between bags in the top tier.

SLOPE WALLS/ EROSION CONTROL

Controlling erosion with rip rap is almost as easy as playing with children's building blocks. Because it will set from natural moisture alone and comes in easy-to-handle bags, erosion walls can be built from rip rap even in locations inaccessible for other construction methods.

Tools and Materials

QUIKRETE® Concrete or Sand Mix
Steel reinforcing rods
Sledgehammer, shovel, rake, and tamper

CONSTRUCTION

1. Place first tier of bags onto a secure base end-to-end.

2. Set back succeeding rows in a stair-step fashion to full height of slope. Set bags in a running bond pattern with the ends butted together and corners interlocked. Anchor the bags to the slope with 3/8″ rebar. Perforate and tamp bags as thoroughly as possible.

Set Bags in a Running Bond Pattern with the Ends Butted Together and Corners Interlocked.

3. As each tier is laid, backfill with tamped-in dirt to assure a solid bank.

For Best Results

Drive steel reinforcing rods through each bag to anchor them to the slope.

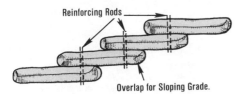

Reinforcing Rods

Overlap for Sloping Grade.

Use 3/8″ Rebar to Anchor Bags.

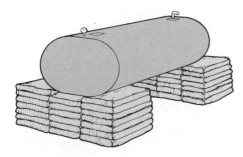

Avoid doing the job when the temperature is at or near freezing.

Complete the job with as little interruption as possible to assure integral construction.

If water is available, keep the material wet for 4 days to assist curing.

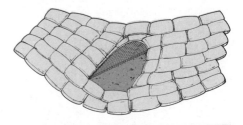

Basic Brick Construction:
Walls, Corners, and Pillars and Posts

The best way to learn the art of bricklaying is through hands-on experience, and there's no better place to start than with a basic freestanding brick wall. The

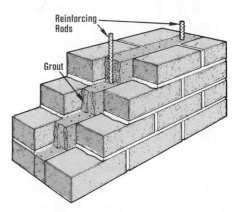

Reinforcing Rods

Grout

wall described here is built in the common or American bond pattern, a pattern that is very strong and easy to lay. The wall is built in two wythes or tiers and can be safely built up to 3'; for a wall above 3', steel reinforcement is required. Reinforcing can be either rods inserted into the grout after it has stiffened slightly or ties laid across two wythes to help hold them together. If you are planning to build a wall more than 3' high, it is best to consult your local building codes for exact specifications and techniques.

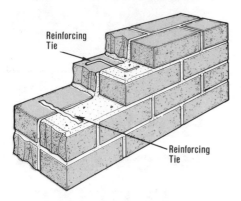

Reinforcing Tie

Reinforcing Tie

BRICKLAYING TERMS

Before beginning any of the bricklaying projects, study the following terms and their definitions. This will help you understand the various brick positions and patterns, as well as the typical mortar joints used.

Bull Header. A rowlock brick laid with its longest dimension perpendicular to the face of the wall.

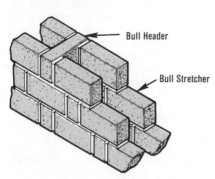

Bull Header

Bull Stretcher

Bull Stretcher. A rowlock brick laid with its longest dimension parallel to the face of the wall.

Course. One of the continuous horizontal rows of masonry that, bonded together, forms the masonry structure.

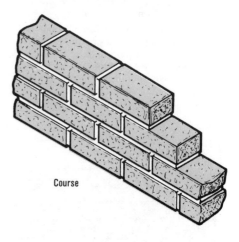

Course

Header. A masonry unit laid flat with its longest dimension perpendicular to the face of the wall. It is generally used to tie two wythes of masonry together.

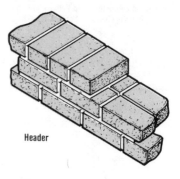

Header

Rowlock. A brick laid on its face, or edge.

Soldier. A brick laid on its end so that its longest dimension is parallel to the vertical axis of the face of the wall.

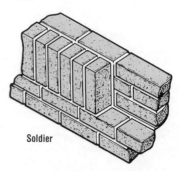

Soldier

Stretcher. A masonry unit laid flat with its longest dimension parallel to the face of the wall.

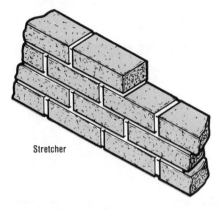

Stretcher

Wythe. A continuous vertical section or thickness of masonry 4″ or greater.

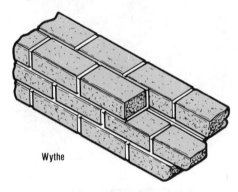

Wythe

BRICK WALLS

Tools and Materials

QUIKRETE® Mortar Mix
Bricks, chalk line, mortarboard, hose, wheelbarrow, trowel, level, carpenter's square, tape measure, brick set, mason's hammer, goggles, jointer, mason's line, and line blocks

SELECTING A SITE

Take time to select a site for your wall; careful location can contribute greatly to the wall's longevity. Choose a spot where the soil is firm and drainage is good. Whenever possible, avoid locating the wall near large trees because the roots can exert great pressure on the wall and easily crack the foundation.

PREPARATION

The first step in building a brick wall is to lay a solid footer or foundation wall. For detailed instructions on pouring a concrete footer or foundation, see *Footers for Walls* (page 9) or *Concrete Walls* (page 9). Be sure to allow the footer or foundation at least two full days to cure before beginning to lay the brick.

Locate your bricks in several stacks along the jobsite; this will save you time and effort later. To prevent the bricks from absorbing too much moisture from the mortar, hose them down a few hours before beginning work. The hose will also come in handy for rinsing your tools occasionally as you work and for keeping the mortar sufficiently moist.

To locate the outer edge of the wall, use a tape measure to measure in from the edge of the foundation at each end. Snap a chalk line between the two points to mark a guideline to keep the wall centered. You are now ready to begin building the wall using the following step-by-step procedure.

PREPARING THE MORTAR

1. Mix the QUIKRETE® Mortar Mix with water until you obtain a smooth, plastic-like consistency.

Divide the mortar cleanly with the trowel; do not scrape it. Good furrows not only ensure that the bricks are laid evenly, but they also help to squeeze out excess mortar on the sides as the bricks are set in place.

LAYING THE BRICKS

1. Lay the first course of stretcher bricks in the mortar. Beginning with the second brick, apply mortar to the head joint end of each brick, then shove the bricks into place firmly so that the mortar is squeezed out of all sides of the joints. Use a level to check the course for correct height, then place it on top to make sure that all the bricks are plumb and level.

2. Make a dry run by laying a course of stretcher bricks along the chalk line for the entire length of the wall. Leave 1/2" between each brick for the head joints and mark the position of the bricks on the foundation with a piece of chalk. Lay this course without cutting any of the bricks; if necessary, adjust the head joint width.

3. Remove the dry course from the foundation, then throw a mortar line on the foundation. To do this, load the trowel with mortar and, as you bring your arm back toward your body, rotate the trowel to deposit the mortar evenly. Mortar should be applied approximately 1" thick, 1 brick wide, and 3 to 4 bricks long. (You might want to practice throwing lines on the mortarboard until you become familiar with the technique.)

4. Furrow the mortar with the point of the trowel using a stippling motion.

2. Make sure that the head joint thicknesses correspond with your chalk marks. When you have to move a brick, tap it gently with the trowel handle; never pull on it because this breaks the bond. Be sure to trim off any excess mortar from the sides of the bricks.

3. Throw another mortar line alongside the first course, then begin laying the second, or backup, course. Use the level to make sure that the two courses are of equal height, but do not mortar them together.

4. Before beginning to lay the second, or header, course, cut two bricks to half length. To cut a brick, lay it on the ground and score it all the way around using a hammer and brick set. Break the brick in two with a sharp blow to the brick set. **Note:** When cutting bricks, protect your eyes by wearing goggles.

5. Use the two half bricks to begin the second, or header, course. This will ensure that the first two courses are staggered for structural purposes.

6. To finish the second course of the lead, lay three header bricks and make sure that they are plumb and level. As seen in the photo, the third and fifth courses consist of stretchers similar to the first course; the fourth course begins with a single header, followed by stretchers. Use the level to make sure that the lead is true on each course.

7. Build another lead on the other end of the foundation. As the mortar begins to set, it is best to stop laying bricks and use a concave jointer to finish the mortar joints. Work along the vertical joints first; this will help make them weatherproof as well as improve the appearance of the wall.

FILLING IN THE LEADS

1. Stretch a mason's line between the completed leads, then begin laying the outer course. The line should be approximately 1/16″ away from the bricks and flush with their top edges as shown. Work from both ends of the wall toward the middle. When you reach the final brick, mortar both sides of it and push it straight down to squeeze the mortar out from the joints.

2. Move the mason's line to the back of the wall and begin laying the backup course. Remember to check your work with the level for accuracy and finish the joints with the concave jointer when they are almost dry.

3. The fifth, or top, course is laid exactly like the first. Move the mason's line up, throw a mortar line, and begin laying the bricks. Apply a generous amount of mortar on the face of each brick, then shove the brick firmly into place.

4. To build a higher wall, simply build more five-course leads at each end of the wall. Keep in mind that some type of reinforcing should be used for higher walls.

5. Scoop mortar onto the trowel and use the concave jointer to fill in the joints on the top course. Keep a careful check on the joint thickness as you go. When you have laid the last brick, check the top course for alignment.

BUILDING CORNERS

A wall with corners is not much harder to build than the basic freestanding wall. The following directions show how to build a corner in the common bond pattern, but they can be adapted to any of the other patterns as well.

1. Snap chalk lines on both sides, then check to make sure that they are perfectly square using a carpenter's square or the 3-4-5 method.

2. Make a dry run to mark the position of the bricks. Throw a mortar line, then place the first brick exactly at the corner, being careful to line it up with the chalk lines.

3. Lay the four remaining bricks in the first course of the lead. With the level and/or carpenter's square, check the alignment and make sure that the bricks are level and plumb.

4. Throw mortar lines and lay the back-up course as shown. Both courses should be level with one another; there is no mortar joint between the two.

5. To lay the second course, cut two bricks into quarter and three-quarter pieces. Begin by laying the three-quarter brick pieces perpendicular to one another to form the outer edge of the corner. Continue by laying several header bricks out from the corner. Finally, complete the second course by inserting the two quarter closure bricks as shown.

6. Lay courses 3 through 5 to finish the corner lead. Courses 3 and 5 are similar to course 1; course 4 begins with a header positioned as shown.

7. Construct a second lead at the opposite corner.

this is a variation of the running bond, with a course of full-length headers placed at regular intervals for structural bonding.

Flemish Bond. This pattern uses alternate stretchers and headers, with the headers in alternate courses centered over the stretchers in the intervening courses.

Flemish Bond

OTHER TYPES OF BONDS

In addition to the common bond pattern, there are a number of other patterns from which to choose. By using the previous directions for laying the common bond, you can use any of these patterns to give variety to your bricklaying work.

Running Bond. This is the simplest pattern; it consists of only stretchers. Reinforcing ties are usually used with it because of the absence of headers. Running bond is common in brick veneer walls and wall cavity construction.

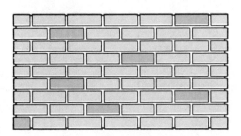

Running Bond

Common or American Bond. As detailed in the step-by-step instructions,

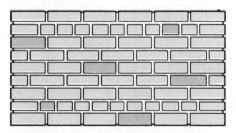

Common Bond

English Bond. This pattern also uses alternate stretchers and headers, but the headers are centered on the stretchers and the joints between the stretchers. The head joints between the stretchers in all the courses line up vertically.

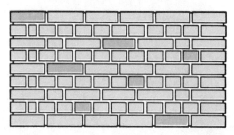

English Bond

English Cross or Dutch Bond. This is a variation on the English, the only difference being that the vertical joints between the stretchers in alternate courses do not line up vertically.

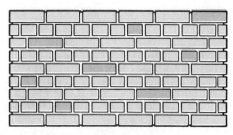

English Cross

These joints center on the stretchers themselves.

Stack or Block Bond. This is a weak bond, used normally for decorative effect on veneers. All vertical joints are aligned, and steel reinforcing ties must be installed if the pattern is being used structurally.

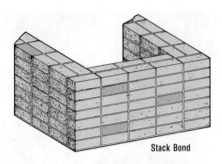

Stack Bond

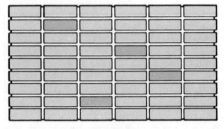

Stack Bond

JOINTS

There are several commonly used methods of finishing mortared joints. Choose a finishing method based on the type of construction. The best joints for strength and waterproofing are concave and V-joints. A weathered joint is also strong and the most watertight. Raked, struck, and extruded joints are perhaps the most dramatic looking; however, they are not very water-resistant. Care should be taken when using them in rainy or freezing climates. A flush joint is the simplest joint—excess mortar is simply cut off with the trowel. But this joint is not particularly strong or water-resistant.

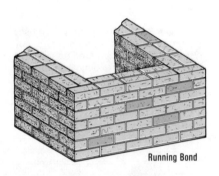

Running Bond

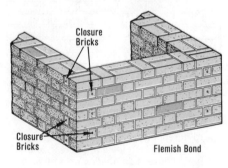

Flemish Bond

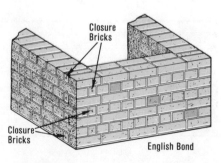

English Bond

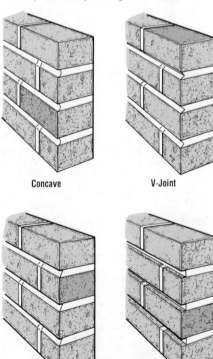

Concave   V-Joint

Weathered   Raked

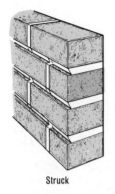

Struck   **Extruded**

The Following Figures Illustrate Bond Patterns for Solid Piers. Alternate the Courses as Shown for Narrow Posts.

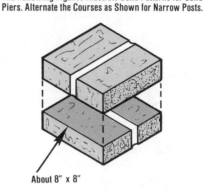

About 8" x 8"

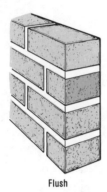

Flush

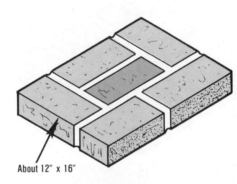

About 12" x 16"

PILLARS AND POSTS

The first step in making pillars and posts of masonry units is to construct adequate footings.

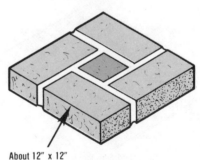

About 12" x 12"

1. Make the forms. If the top surface of the footings will be level with or below the grade, cut the forms directly in the soil. If the surface of the footing will be above grade, use a shallow wood form in conjunction with a cavity cut in the soil.

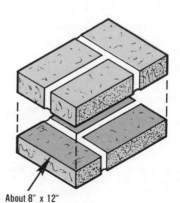

About 8" x 12"

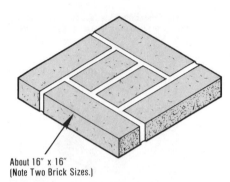

About 16" x 16"
(Note Two Brick Sizes.)

Second. Fourth. Sixth. etc.. Courses

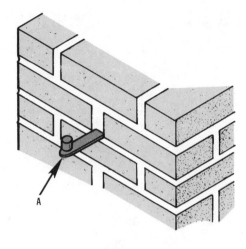

A

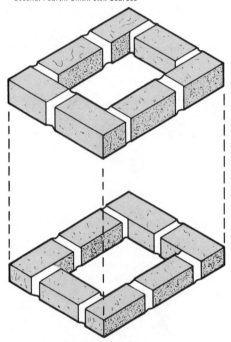

First. Third. Fifth. etc.. Courses

Bond Pattern for a Hollow Pier.
Alternate Courses.

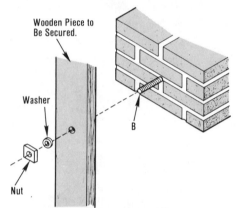

Wooden Piece to
Be Secured.

Washer

B

Nut

To Mount a Gate, either (A) Install Hinge Hooks by
Mortaring Them into Joints, or (B) Attach a Wood
Frame to Bolts Mortared into the Post.

2. Mix QUIKRETE® Concrete Mix and
   pour it into the form.

3. When all standing water has evaporated, use a trowel to smooth the surface of the footing.

4. Moist-cure the concrete.

Once the footings have set, continue
pillar and post construction as you would
if you were building a full wall. Use a level frequently to check the horizontal
plane of each course and the plumbness

of each wall. Use a large carpenter's
square to ensure that the corners are
square. Cap the pillar or post with precast concrete slabs, hand-formed
mounds of QUIKRETE® Concrete or
Mortar, removable wood caps, or pieces
of flagstone.

Typical Post Caps.

Precast Slab

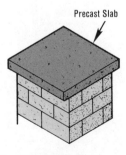

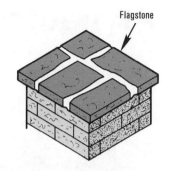

Flagstone

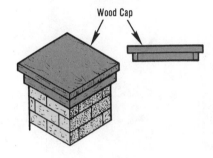

Wood Cap

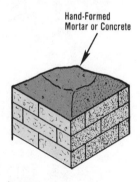

Hand-Formed
Mortar or Concrete

For Best Results

Be sure that dirt walls are vertical or that they slant out slightly at the base.

Be sure that the base for the footing is firm and level.

Check to see that the surface of the wood form is level.

Add vertical steel reinforcement rods or conduit for electrical cable.

Add brackets, bolts, studs, hinges, light fixtures, and/or hangers before the concrete or masonry has set.

Install the cap at a slight angle so that it sheds water.

Gallery of Brick Projects

Once you've learned the basics of working with brick, you can use your knowledge to build a variety of projects. From simple lawn edging to ornate entryways, brick lends a distinctive touch to your home's exterior.

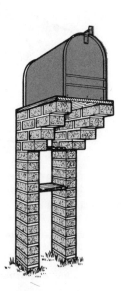

Brick Steps

As an alternative to plain concrete steps, bricks can be used as facing over the concrete. Building brick steps involves the same tools and materials as concrete steps, with the following additions: QUIKRETE® Mortar Mix, bricks, 1/2" wooden spacer, concave jointer, wooden mallet, mason's line, burlap sack, and stiff broom or brush.

Follow the same procedures that are used for concrete steps to prepare the base, build the forms, pour the concrete, finish the surface, and cure the concrete. You are now ready to lay the bricks in the concrete, using the following procedure:

1. Wet down the bricks several hours before beginning the project; this will prevent them from absorbing too much water from the mortar.

2. Place and screed a 1/2" thick wet mortar bed between temporary form boards set one brick length apart. Use a special bladed screed to level the concrete. The screed rides on the forms and extends down one brick-thickness below them; the forms should be set for this depth, plus an extra 1/2" to allow for the mortar bed.

3. As the screed is moved along, place the bricks in the wet concrete, leaving 1/2" open joints between them. A 1/2" wooden spacer can be used to ensure that the joints are uniform. Gently tap the bricks with a wooden mallet to set them.

4. Use a trowel to pack the concrete into the joints, then tool the joints with a concave jointer.

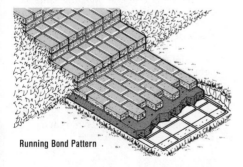

Running Bond Pattern

5. Wait several hours, then scrub the set bricks with a burlap sack to remove any stains. Once the mortar is dry, brush the surface with a stiff broom or brush to remove any bits of dry mortar.

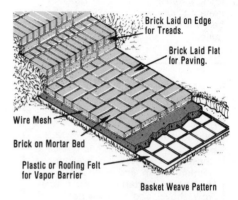

Brick Laid on Edge for Treads.
Brick Laid Flat for Paving.
Wire Mesh
Brick on Mortar Bed
Plastic or Roofing Felt for Vapor Barrier
Basket Weave Pattern

The brick steps in this example were laid in the traditional running bond pattern. Another popular choice is the basket weave pattern, with the bricks either laid flat or on edge as shown in the illustrations.

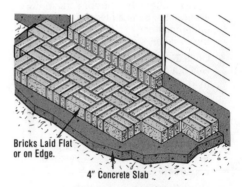

Bricks Laid Flat or on Edge.
4" Concrete Slab

Tree Wells

Trees can be severely damaged when a site is regraded. Roots might be exposed when the ground level is lowered, and raising a site more than 8" can cut off needed light, air, and water. In either case, the tree could die.

The solution is to build a tree well, maintaining a circle of ground next to the tree at the level existing before regrading. Not only will a tree well help the tree, it will also make your yard more attractive.

RAISED TREE WELLS

Physically, a tree well is nothing more than a retaining wall. When the ground is cut away, a raised well keeps the surrounding soil at its original level. Stone, brick, or block can be used, or a concrete wall can be poured. The brick well below is effective, attractive, and easy to build.

Tools and Materials

QUIKRETE® Concrete Mix
QUIKRETE® Mortar Mix
Brick
Plywood template
Brick trowel, brick hammer, brick set, mason's rule, 4' level, convex and flat jointers, brush, and screed
Mixing box, mortarboard, wheelbarrow, shovel, and masonry hoe

---

SITE PREPARATION

1. After determining the well size, lay a length of garden hose or rope around the tree where the interior edge of the well will be. Slide a piece of plywood under the hose and mark the arc of the circle on the wood.

2. Cut a 2'- to 3'-long template for the well out of the plywood. The arc will mark the front edge of the template.

3. Excavate a 16"-wide trench, beginning about 4" inside the hose. Dig the trench to several inches below the frost line, keeping the bottom 6" of the trench as smooth as possible so that a footer can be poured without constructing forms.

4. Using the prepared concrete mix, pour a 6" footer. Screed it smooth, and level. Cure it for at least 1 day.

BUILDING THE WELL

1. Dry-lay 2 wythes of brick around the footer, keeping 1/2" joints between the wythes and bricks. The wythes are laid in a horizontal running bond so that head joints do not extend through the width of the wall. Mark the location of the bricks on the footer.

2. Remove the bricks and lay a 1/2" bed of the prepared mortar mix on the footer. Prepare only as much mortar as can be used in an hour.

3. Lay the first course in the mortar bed—do not butter the head joints or the joints between the wythes. These are left open so moisture can escape and to prevent cracks in the wall. Plumb and level each brick, using the template to keep the well plumb from point to point.

4. Using 1/2" bed joints and a vertical running bond in each wythe, build up the well to the former ground level. Plumb and level as you go.

5. After each course is laid, clean out any mortar that falls into the head joints. Use metal ties to bond the wythes together every 5 to 6 courses.

6. Tool the joints with the convex jointer as they are setting up. After the joints harden, brush out any loose mortar.

7. Lay the top course with headers, buttering both sides of the bricks before laying them. Tool the top joints flat to prevent moisture entry.

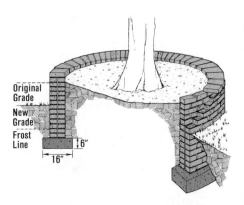

SUNKEN TREE WELL

To keep the tree's root system close to necessary nutrients when the ground level is raised, a sunken tree well is constructed. Site preparation is the same as described earlier; well construction can also be done according to the method already described, except that for a sunken tree well, *all* joints are mortared, and the exterior face of the well is parged with cement up to the grade line.

A simple alternative to brick construction, which can be used for either raised or sunken wells, is mortarless block construction with QUIKWALL® Surface Bonding Cement. (See page 83).

Concrete Block Construc- tion

Use QUIKRETE® Mortar Mix to lay a concrete block wall as shown.

Tools and Materials

QUIKRETE® Mortar Mix
Concrete block
Mason's line, line blocks, 4' level, brick trowel, jointer, mason's hammer, and stiff brush
Mixing board, hoe, and mortarboard

LAYING THE FIRST COURSE

1. Excavate the site and construct the footing. (See pages 2 and 41.)

2. Locate the corners of the wall on the footing. Dry-lay the first course of blocks, leaving space for the mortar. Snap a chalk line to mark the position of the blocks on the footing.

3. Pick up the blocks and spread a full bed of QUIKRETE® Mortar Mix on the footing. Use a trowel to furrow the mortar.

4. Position the corner block carefully, with the thicker end of the face shell-up; all blocks should be laid this way to provide a larger mortar bedding area. When handling a block, always tip it slightly toward you so that you can see the edge of the course below.

5. Place several blocks on end and apply mortar to their vertical face shells. Push each block down into the mortar bed and against the previously laid block. Joints should be about 3/8" thick.

6. After three or four blocks have been laid, use a level to check for plumbness and correct alignment. Make any adjustments by tapping the block with the trowel handle, then complete the first course. Make *all* adjustments while the mortar is still soft.

LAYING THE REMAINING COURSES

1. With the remaining courses, mortar is applied to the horizontal face shells of each block; for the vertical joints, mortar either the previously laid block or the block to be placed, but not both. As each block is laid, cut off the excess mortar with the trowel.

2. When laying the remainder of the wall, the corners should be built first, usually 4 or 5 courses at a time. As each course is laid at the corner, it should be stepped back a half block. Check for plumbness, alignment, and horizontal spacing of the blocks.

3. To fill in the wall between corners, stretch a mason's line from corner to corner and lay the top outside edge of the blocks against it. When placing the closure block, all edges of the opening and all four vertical edges of the closure block should be buttered with mortar. Make sure all joints are tight and weatherproof.

4. Work the joints after each section of the wall has been laid, and the mortar has partially hardened. Tool the horizontal joints first, then work the vertical joints with an S-shaped jointer.

5. Wood plates can be fastened to the top course. Use 1/2"-diameter, 18"-long anchor bolts in the cores of the top 2 courses, no more than 4' apart. Fill the cores with mortar, making sure that the bolts extend a few inches above the top of the wall.

For Best Results

Use QUIKRETE® Masonry Coating to waterproof both above and below the grade line.

DECORATIVE BLOCK SCREEN WALL

A decorative block wall is an attractive change from a solid wall. Basic construction techniques do not vary much from those for solid block walls, but a strong footing must be provided to avoid cracks that will seriously weaken the wall.

Tools and Materials

QUIKRETE® Mortar Mix
Decorative concrete block
Mixing board, hoe, and hawk
Mason's line, line blocks, 4' level,
  brick trowel, jointer, and stiff brush

LAYING THE SCREEN WALL

1. Construct a footing one block length longer than the wall. (Refer to page 9.)

2. Drive a stake into the ground at the end of the footer opposite the end where wall construction will begin. The leading edge of the stake is placed on the front line of the wall, with a nail driven into it at the exact height of the first course.

3. Set the opposite end block in place. Using a line block, attach a mason's line from the end block to the nail in the stake. Dry-lay the first course of blocks along the line, leaving 1/2" joints between the blocks. Mark the location of the blocks on the footer.

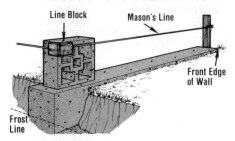

4. Lay a 1/2" bed of the prepared mortar mix along the footer and lay the first course from the end opposite the stake. By laying the course from end to end, rather than building the corners first, the first course can be off an inch or two without having to cut a closure block.

5. Butter the ends of each block before setting it in place, making certain to set the blocks level.

6. The remaining courses are laid similarly to the first course, using the vertical joints in the bottom course as guides. Butter the ends and bottom of blocks in the upper courses before placing them. Use the level to check alignment every 3 to 4 blocks and to check plumb every 2 to 3 courses.

7. Strike the joints after the mortar begins to harden; use a stiff-bristled brush to remove any loose particles of mortar.

8. Moist-cure the mortar for 3 to 4 days by misting the wall with a fine spray several times daily.

For Best Results

Mineral pigments can be added to the mortar mix to match the color of the block. For more information on colored finishes, refer to page 39.

Stone Masonry:
Garden, Patio, Driveway Walls

Low maintenance requirements and indefinite durability make stone masonry as financially appealing as it is visually attractive. There are two principal styles. Ashlar, or cut stone, creates a formal effect and is frequently used in the construction of commercial and similar buildings. Rubblestone construction has a more rustic appearance because the stone is either not cut at all or receives only a rough cut. Either style can be laid in courses or at random, with or without mortar. However, ashlar is easier to work with because the shapes are more even. For the same reason, ashlar is also much more expensive than rubblestone. An ashlar project of almost any size requires that the stone be purchased rather than cut by you, while rubblestone may be laid up just as you find it, free in the fields.

In addition to the projects that follow, consider building such things as planters, tree wells, barbecue pits, and fireplaces from stone. Even structural walls can take advantage of stone's endurance and beauty with careful construction techniques. But whatever your project, stone construction demands a heavy pair of work gloves, boots, and, unless your job will require absolutely no stone cutting, a pair of safety glasses or goggles.

ASHLAR DRIVEWAY WALL (MORTARED)

FOOTER CONSTRUCTION

1. Stake out an area for a footer 4" to 5" beyond the wall edge on all sides. Excavate deep enough to allow an 8" to 10" footer to be sunk below the frost line.

2. Construct the form for the footer out of the scrap lumber. Pour the footer with QUIKRETE® Concrete Mix (see page 10).

Tools and Materials

QUIKRETE® Concrete and Mortar (Masonry) Mix
2 × 4 or 2 × 8 scrap lumber, nails, and claw or ball peen hammer
Stone (1 ton = approximately 50 to 60 square feet, 6" thick)
Mason's hammer, 2-lb. mash hammer, plain stone chisel, 2' level, 2' square, mason's modular rule, 50' steel tape, slicker jointer, pointing trowel, ball of line, line pins, and brush
Mixing box, shovel, hoe, mortarboard, wheelbarrow, bucket, and hose

---

3. If the wall is to be constructed into a slope, step the footer as shown in order to save on concrete.

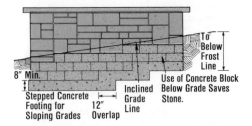

8" Min.
Stepped Concrete Footing for Sloping Grades
12" Overlap
Inclined Grade Line
To Below Frost Line
Use of Concrete Block Below Grade Saves Stone.

4. Depending on how far below grade the footer must be sunk in order to be beneath the frost line, stone can be saved by using concrete blocks to bring the foundation up to the grade level as shown in the diagram. Fill the hollows in the blocks with stone chips and mortar to make a firm base for laying the stone.

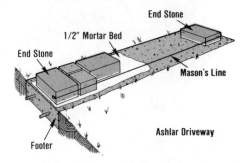

End Stone
1/2" Mortar Bed
End Stone
Mason's Line
Ashlar Driveway
Footer

WALL CONSTRUCTION

1. Cure the footer for 3 to 4 days before constructing the wall. Set a large stone, approximately as wide as the wall, at each end of the footer. Attach line blocks to the outside corners of

each stone and run the mason's line between them to keep wall alignment.

2. The wall is laid up in two wythes, working from the ends toward the middle of the wall. Dry-lay stones first to obtain proper placement; remember to leave 1/2" head joints between the stones.

3. Lay a 1/2" mortar bed along the footer and begin building the wall. Mix only as much mortar as will be used in about an hour. Build from the ends toward the center, buttering the head joints before setting the stone in place. On wider walls the cavity between the wythes is filled with stone chips and mortar as the wall is built.

4. Depending on whether the stone is being laid in a random or coursed pattern, the stonework is laid up in successive tiers, or courses, to the full height of the wall. Work both wythes simultaneously, filling the cavity as you go.

5. Lay end stones on each row first so that the line can be raised with the wall to keep it straight. The stone is plumbed "bump to bump" because the faces are not smooth like brick.

6. Lay two smaller stones against a larger one (called a *two against one*) at intervals to strengthen the wall.

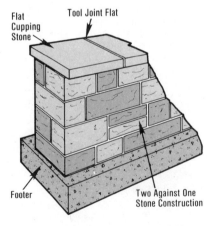

Flat Cupping Stone
Tool Joint Flat
Footer
Two Against One Stone Construction

7. Lay large, thin stones on top as capping. The joints are tooled flat to prevent moisture entry.

FINISHING MORTAR

1. Rake out the joints to a depth of 1/2" after the mortar has set slightly to highlight the stone edges. Use the slicker jointer to do this.

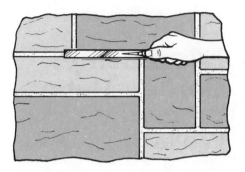

2. Brush out the joints after the mortar is dry enough not to smear.

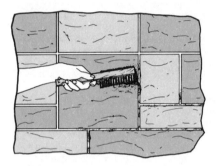

For Best Results

Check local requirements before beginning the project. Many municipalities require a building permit and engineer's approval for any wall more than 3' high.

To make the foundation more secure, lay parallel 3/8" reinforcing rods lengthwise in the footer and install a 3" gravel drainage bed against it.

Clean bedding faces of the stones of all dirt, soil, and vegetable matter before they are laid so that a strong mortar bond is made.

Use small wooden wedges beneath large stones; their weight might squeeze the mortar out of the joints. After the mortar stiffens, remove the wedges and pack the holes with mortar or QUIKRETE® Quick-Setting Cement.

If lighting fixtures are to be mounted on the wall, lay the conduit in the wythe cavity at the desired height as work progresses.

Overhang the capping stones 1" from the sides of the wall as a drip edge.

RUBBLESTONE WALLS

Rubblestone construction will blend a wall naturally with a surrounding lawn or landscape. Care in selecting and laying the stones must be taken if you are going to use a coursed pattern.

Tools and Materials

QUIKRETE® Concrete Mix and Mortar (Masonry) Mix
2 × 4 or 2 × 8 scrap lumber, nails, and claw or ball peen hammer
Stone
Stone sledgehammer, 2-lb. mash hammer, bricklayer's trowel, pointing trowel, slicker jointer, 50' steel tape, 4' level, ball of line, brush, batter board, plain stone chisel, pointing chisel, and rolling bead jointer (if desired)
Mixing box, shovel, hoe, wheelbarrow, and mortarboard

BASE CONSTRUCTION

1. Follow steps 1 through 4 in the preceding section.

2. The wall is constructed after the footer has cured for 3 to 4 days. Begin by laying a large stone, approximately as wide as the wall, at each end of the footer. The mortar bed should be thick enough so that the stone rests completely in it, but should not be deeper than 2".

3. String a line between stakes placed at the wall line on each end of the footer. The face of each stone should be no more than 1" from the string.

4. Lay the first course in two wythes within the guides, keeping the bed and head joints no more than 2" thick. Use care in selecting the stones so that a larger joint is not required. Larger stones should be used at the bottom of the wall for stability. They will also be easier to position there.

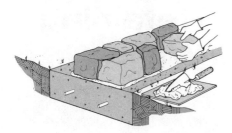

5. On wider walls and where stones cannot be fitted without leaving a gap of 2" or less, use stone chips and mortar to fill cavities.

6. Stones of approximate wall-width are laid across the wall at intervals. Bondstones, as they are called, should be placed so that there is one for every 6 to 10 square feet of wall surface to tie the wall together.

BUILDING THE WALL

1. Both wythes are worked simultaneously in building up the wall to its full height, with larger stones at lower levels and smaller stones toward the top. Slope the wall inward on both sides 1" for each foot of vertical rise. Use a batter board, which can be built out of scrap wood, to keep the wall plumb.

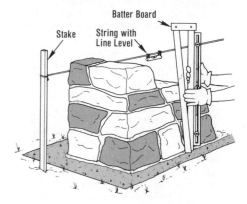

Batter Board
Stake
String with Line Level

2. Lay end stones first and work toward the middle of the wall. Dry-lay the stones first to obtain proper placement before laying down the mortar. Head joints between stones are not buttered as with brick. Instead, after the stone is set in the mortar bed, mortar is slushed into the head joints between the stones.

3. Periodically lay two smaller stones against a larger one (called a *two against one*) as each course is laid out. Also, periodically overlap stones. In addition to creating a more natural look, these methods create a firmer bond within the wall.

4. As each course is laid, fill in the cavity between wythes before proceeding to the next course. Bondstones should be set in each course.

5. Broad, thinner stones are laid on top as capping. If possible, they should project 1" on all sides as a drip edge.

Tool the joints flat to prevent moisture from entering.

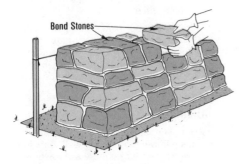

Bond Stones

FINISHING THE JOINTS

1. Rake out the wall joints 1/2" to 3/4" thick after the mortar has achieved a slight set. Smooth the joints flat with the slicker jointer (use pointing trowel for broader joints) to highlight the stone edges.

2. Brush any loose mortar particles from the joints after it is hard enough to be brushed without smearing.

3. As an alternative, a rolling bead joint can be applied to the wall. After the joints have been raked out to 3/4" and brushed, moisten an area that can be pointed within 15 minutes. **DO NOT** soak the joint.

4. Apply fresh mortar to the joint with a rolling bead jointer, which can be purchased or made from a section of 3/4" copper pipe. Apply with a smooth, steady motion from the leading edge of the joint.

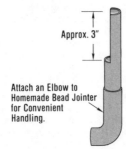

Approx. 3"

Attach an Elbow to Homemade Bead Jointer for Convenient Handling.

5. Blend the joints as smoothly as possible at intersections so that the joints appear unbroken. Going over a joint already laid might pull it away onto the jointer.

6. Brush joints lightly with a soft brush after they have hardened.

For Best Results

Clean all faces of stone before laying them. Dirt, soil, and vegetable matter will prevent the mortar and stone from bonding.

Check local ordinances. Many municipalities require a building permit and an engineer's approval before a wall higher than 3' can be built.

Construct a small section of the wall to use as a rough gauge of how much mortar to mix and how much will be needed for building the rest of the wall.

The weight of large stones can squeeze mortar out of their bedding joints. Insert small wooden wedges under the stones when they are laid. After the mortar has set enough to hold the weight, remove the wedges and pack the holes with mortar or QUIKRETE® Quick-Setting Cement.

If stones are in short supply, use concrete blocks to bring the foundation up to the front grade level.

Be sure to keep your tools slightly damp while pointing in order to ease the work. Wipe excess mortar off the tools after each application.

Brick, Block, and Stone Retaining Walls

As with the concrete retaining walls discussed on page 14, brick, block, and stone retaining walls protect your property from soil erosion while, at the same time, add distinction to your home's exterior. The building procedures are the same as those used in basic wall construction; refer to the *Footers, Basic Brick Construction, Concrete Block Construction,* and *Stone Masonry* sections for details. The tools and materials needed are also identical to those necessary for basic wall construction, with the following additions: 1" plastic pipe (for drainage); QUIKRETE® Masonry Coating (for coating the brick and block walls); and a screen (for covering the pipe on the stone wall).

BUILDING THE WALLS

1. Before beginning work on any retaining wall, check local ordinances and building codes. Many municipalities require a building permit and an engineer's approval before a wall higher than 3' can be built.

2. For added structural integrity in the brick retaining wall, insert steel rebars between the wythes as shown in the illustration. Pour a wet mixture of

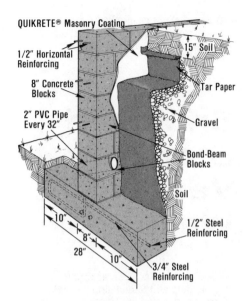

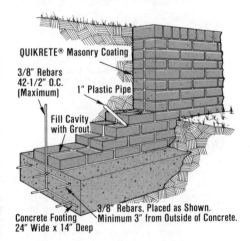

QUIKRETE® Mortar Mix between the wythes to bond the rebars. On the concrete block wall, use rebars in the block cavities for horizontal reinforcement. Additional reinforcement is not necessary on the stone wall because it is built lower to the ground than the other walls.

3. Because weep holes are essential for proper drainage, a length of plastic pipe must be installed approximately every 6' along the retaining walls. Notch the brick/block to accommo-

date the pipes and use mortar to secure them as shown in the illustrations. On the stone walls, slope the pipe downward toward the front of the wall, about 8" above the front grade; this will help prevent pressure buildup against the back of the wall. Place a screen over the back opening and pile broken stone over the screen to prevent the pipe from becoming clogged.

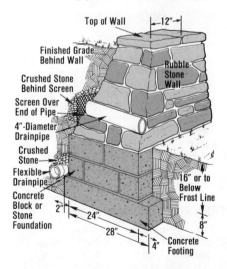

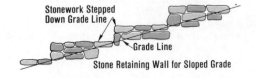

Stone Retaining Wall for Sloped Grade

4. Brush a coat of QUIKRETE® Masonry Coating on the back of the finished brick and block walls to make them watertight.

Brick and Stone Veneer Walls

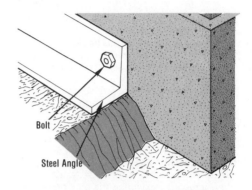

Bolt

Steel Angle

Veneer masonry is a popular choice for home building and remodeling, because it gives the appearance of a solid brick or stone wall while providing better economy and insulation. It can be used as an addition to conventional wood frame structures, and can also be placed on concrete block walls. Depending on personal preference, it may cover an entire wall from foundation to roof, or it can stop at windowsill level.

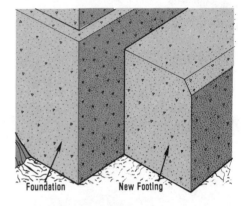

Foundation　　New Footing

Tools and Materials

QUIKRETE® Mortar Mix
Bricks or stones, gravel or crushed stone, reinforcing rebar, forming lumber and stakes (optional, needed only if making new forms), flashing, sheathing, galvanized metal wall ties, masonry nails or stud gun, rubber hose, and story pole
Steel angle (optional), pickax, square-faced shovel, trowel, tamper, saw, wooden wedges, screed, and level

PREPARING THE FOUNDATION

If the footing of the house extends out 6" or more, the veneer can rest directly on top of it. If the footing is less than 6", it must be "extended" before the veneer can be placed on it. To "extend" the footing, either bolt a corrosion-resistant steel angle to the existing foundation, or pour a new footing next to the foundation. (See page 9 for footer construction details.) If you are making a new footing,

pour it to within a few inches of ground level, then start the veneer at that point. The veneer must always be tied to the old foundation; to ensure a good bond, wash the old foundation surface, and coat it with grout.

LAYING A BRICK VENEER WALL

1. Install flashing over the footing to prevent water from seeping behind the veneer. Copper, aluminum, lead, or roofing paper may be used for this. Spread a 1/2" bed of mortar on top of the footing, then push the flashing down firmly into it. (It is a good idea to install flashing at the heads and sills of doors and windows as well.)

2. Cover the existing siding with a good sheathing material, such as tarpaper. Always leave a 1" air space between the sheathing and the veneer.

3. To lay the first course of bricks, use a trowel to spread a 1"-thick bed of mortar on top of the flashing. Tap each brick into place with the trowel handle; never pull on a brick, because this can break the bond. Make sure that all the bricks are plumb and level.

4. To hold the veneer in place, nail galvanized metal wall ties through the siding and into the studs. Space the ties every 32″ horizontally and every 16″ vertically, and offset the rows so that the ties do not line up.

5. Make weep holes, approximately 24″ on center, in the vertical joints of the first course of bricks. To form the weep holes, use short lengths of rubber hose, which can be easily removed after the mortar has set. The weep holes will act as a drainage system to allow any water that may seep in in spite of the slashing to escape.

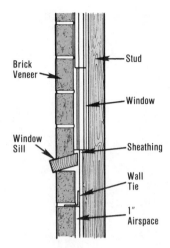

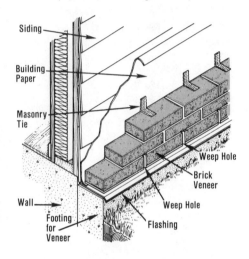

with the head of the window or door; it must overlap the bricks by 3″ to 4″ on both sides of the window or door.

6. Continue laying each course of bricks, being careful to maintain the precise mortar joint thickness needed to obtain the desired wall height. A story pole may be helpful for accuracy.

7. When you reach a windowsill, lay the bricks on edge in "rowlock" fashion as shown in the illustration. The bricks should also be installed on a slant in the direction of the rainfall. For bricks being laid above windows and doors, a steel lintel must be used as a base. The lintel is set onto the course, even

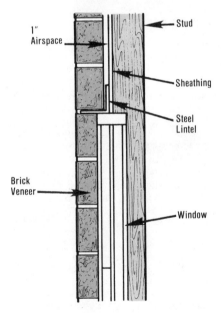

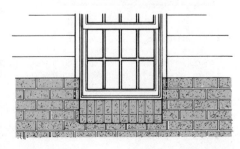

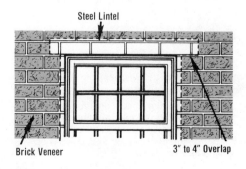

8. If the veneer is being carried all the way to the roof, it must meet the cornice. The frieze board on the cornice should overlap the top course of bricks by at least 1/2". Use 2 × 4 blocking to provide a sound nailing surface for the frieze board.

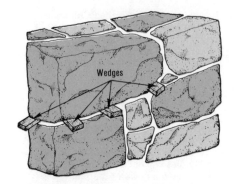

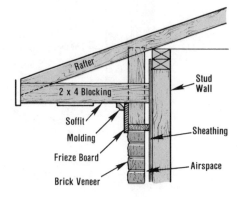

LAYING A STONE VENEER WALL

When laying stone veneer on a concrete block wall, the procedure is very similar to the laying of a brick veneer wall:

1. With masonry nails or a stud gun, attach wall ties to the wall every 2 or 3 square feet. (If the concrete block wall is being built from scratch, insert the ties in the mortar joints between the blocks.)

2. Attach the stones to each other and to the wall with mortar. Lay a 1" mortar bed on the footer, and then begin setting the first course of stones; unless you are using a high grade of dressed stone, you will also be setting small stones or gravel in mortar to fill the irregular, open spaces where the large stones do not meet. For each new course, build up a mortar bed and set the stones in place, checking the alignment as you go. Bend as many of the ties as possible into the joints between the stones.

3. Because very large stones can squeeze out all the mortar in their joints, support them temporarily with wooden wedges. When the mortar has set, pull out the wedges and fill the holes with mortar.

4. When a section has been laid, use a piece of wood to rake out the joints to a depth of 1/2" to 3/4". This will enhance the play of light and shadow on the face of the wall.

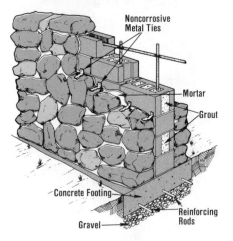

Barbecues

A barbecue is a useful and attractive addition to any backyard, whether it's contemporary styled brick or rustic cobblestone. It should be located, whenever possible, in a corner of a patio to ensure a solid base.

BRICK BARBECUE

Tools and Materials

QUIKRETE® Concrete Mix
QUIKRETE® Mortar Mix
Stakes and nails, form tube, and sand
Square-faced shovel, wheelbarrow, trowel, and level
Bricks, brick set, mason's hammer, 3/8" × 2" steel bar, drill, and 2 × 4 forming lumber

PREPARING THE FOUNDATION AND POURING THE FOOTINGS

To begin the project, measure and stake off the desired area. The perimeter for the barbecue's pit should be approximately 3' × 3'. (The walls of the excavation can be used as forms for the concrete, provided the soil is firm enough.)

Set a 22"-diameter cardboard form tube into the center of the excavation, using 2 × 4s to keep it from moving, as shown. The form tube must be long

enough to extend from the bottom of the excavation to a point 26-1/2" above ground. Check to make sure that it is plumb and level, then fill the tube with sand to approximately 2" below the final grade. Pour the prepared concrete mix around the base of the tube, completely filling the trenches, to finish construction of the footings. Screed the footings. Allow 3 to 4 days for the concrete to cure.

LAYING THE INSIDE OF THE BARBECUE

1. Begin laying half-bricks, with the cut ends facing out, around the form tube. Use 1/2" mortar joints. For information on cutting brick, refer to *Basic Brick Construction* on page 41. As you continue laying the half-bricks, be sure to leave an opening for the ash door.

2. When the third course has been completed, install a 3/8" × 2" horizontal steel bar across the opening as shown. This will support the bricks above the opening.

3. When the seventh course has been completed, drill three equally spaced 3/8"-diameter holes in the tube to act as supports for the metal grate. Insert the bent rods as shown, then lay two additional courses.

4. Drill three more 3/8"-diameter holes, insert three rods to act as supports for the grill, then lay the final course of half-bricks. The inside of the barbecue is now complete.

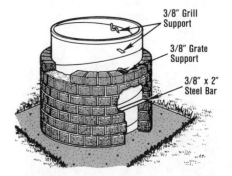

3/8" Grill Support

3/8" Grate Support

3/8" × 2" Steel Bar

LAYING THE OUTSIDE OF THE BARBECUE

1. Lay the first wythe of the rectangular outside wall in a running bond to a height of 4 courses. Build the corners first and work toward the center, using a level to check the plumb and level and to keep the wall aligned.

2. Construct temporary 2 × 4 supports and set them against the brick, flush with the fourth course.

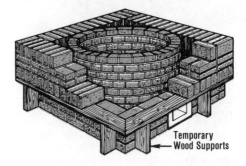

Temporary Wood Supports

3. Lay a course of bull headers.

4. Build 2 wythes of stretchers in a running bond 2 courses high.

5. Lay a course of bull headers level with the height of the pit wall.

6. After the mortar joints begin to set, finish the joints and brush off any loose mortar particles. The top joints are struck flat to prevent moisture entry. Remove the supports after 24 hours.

7. Peel out the form tube down to the sand. Smooth the sand and lay in a 4"

concrete bed, sloping slightly toward the ash opening for water drainage.

8. Fill the spaces between the interior and exterior wall with concrete flush with the brick height. Install the grate and grill. Cure the concrete for 10 days before using the barbecue.

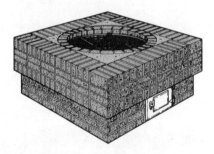

STONE BARBECUE

Stone's sense of mass might at first seem too heavy and imposing for a simple garden barbecue, but its natural qualities work quite well to create an informal, casual air for garden cookouts on a low grill. This barbecue is a relatively easy, economical, and speedy project within the abilities of even the novice do-it-yourselfer. The size of the barbecue will be determined by the dimensions of the grill you choose to use.

Tools and Materials

QUIKRETE® Mortar Mix
QUIKRETE® Concrete Mix
Stainless steel grill
Stone, firebrick, flagstone, trowel, level, mixing box, shovel, hoe, and hawk

CONSTRUCTION

1. Excavate an area 2' wider and 1' longer than the grill, cutting the edges as straight as possible. Dig to a depth of about 4".

2. Pour the prepared concrete mix into the hole and screed it smooth, sloping it slightly away from the end where the fire will be built. Fill to about 1/2" below the ground level. Cure the concrete for 3 to 4 days.

3. Center the grill on the edge of the slab away from where the fire will be built. Mark the edges of the grill on the slab. Remove the grill and lay a 1/2" mortar bed within the marks.

4. Lay a bed of firebrick in the mortar, taking care to keep the bricks straight and to maintain a slight slope toward the edge of the slab. Joints between the bricks should not exceed 3/8". Sweep dry mortar mix into the joints to fill them.

5. Construct the firebrick lining beginning from the outer edges. The brick is built up in 3 courses with mortared joints. Use the level to keep the liner straight and plumb.

6. Construct the stone shell around the liner by setting the base stones in a mortar foundation not thicker than 2". Dry-fit stones before setting them into the mortar. The shell is constructed outward from the liner and built up in courses.

7. After the stones in each course are set in the mortar bed, mortar is slushed into the joints between them to fill the cracks.

8. Construct the sides of the shell 2" to 3" higher than the liner; construct the end 3" to 4" higher than the sides.

9. Spread a mortar bed on top of the shell and lay the flagstone, striking

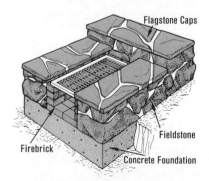

the joints between the stones flat to prevent moisture entry.

For Best Results

Refer to page 41 for more information on laying brick and to page 59 for more information on working with stone.

Lay the flagstone cap with a 1″ overhang as a moisture drip edge.

CONCRETE BLOCK BARBECUE

For an attractive and economical backyard barbecue that is quick and easy to build, yet as sturdy as they come, consider the following one made with concrete blocks and QUIKWALL® Surface Bonding Cement. Or, modify the design to suit your fancy and needs. With the time saved by using QUIKWALL® instead of mortar, you will have plenty of opportunity to exercise your architectural creativity.

Tools and Materials

QUIKRETE® Concrete Mix
QUIKWALL® Surface Bonding Cement
Concrete block
Steel plate, grill, steel hangers, and counterboard
Plasterer's trowel, float, screed, shovel, hoe, mixing box, hawk, and level

CONSTRUCTION

1. Excavate an area 24″ wider and 8″ deeper than the length and combined widths of the grill and counterboard you will use. Dig to a depth of about 4″, keeping the edges as straight as possible.

2. Place the prepared concrete mix in the excavation as a footer. Screed and float. Damp-cure the concrete for 3 to 4 days. (For further information on footers and finishing concrete refer to pages 9 and 36.)

3. Dry-lay the first course of blocks on the footer to determine their correct placement. Begin at one end, interlocking the sidewalls with the back wall. Mark the location of the blocks on the footer.

4. Lay a 1/2″ bed of QUIKWALL® on the footer and set the first course in it, beginning at the same end and butting the blocks together. Make certain that this course is set straight and level.

5. Stack the remaining block in a running bond pattern, interlocking all the walls together. Stack the grill walls 5 courses high, and the counter walls 4 courses high, making certain to place them plumb on the course below.

6. Place the steel hangers in the grill sidewalls after the second, third, and fourth courses; place them in the counter sidewalls after the third course.

7. Mix as much QUIKWALL® as can be used in about an hour and apply a 1/8″-thick coat to completely cover the wall surfaces. After 8 hours, mist the barbecue with a fine spray. Repeat this several times daily for 2 to 3 days to moist-cure.

8. Set the counterboard, steel plate, and grill in place on the hangers.

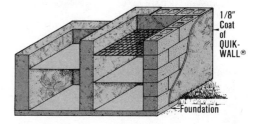

1/8″ Coat of QUIK-WALL®

Foundation

Garden Pools and Fountains

The tranquil beauty and playful shimmer of a reflecting pool or fountain is just the thing to enhance the charm of your garden or patio. Best of all, you can do all the work yourself. Add goldfish or water plants to increase the pool's appeal; fish will even help control the insect population. Future rewards from admiring comments, increased home value, and, not least, your own restful enjoyment will be yours from care and attention now in building your pool.

FREE-FORM CONCRETE POOL

This pool can be given the dimensions and shape you desire, and all you need to build it is simple construction know-how and a few tools.

Tools and Materials

QUIKRETE® Masonry Coating
QUIKRETE® Concrete Mix
Sand
6″ × 6″ wire mesh reinforcement
1″ × 2″ scrap wood
2″ drainpipe and fittings
Shovel, hoe, mixing box, hammer, wooden float or trowel, and brush

CONSTRUCTION

1. Dig a saucer-shaped excavation for the pool with a center 24″ deep.

2. Install the drainpipe at the center of the pool as shown. The coupling should be 6″ above the soil bed. The pipe end is connected to a drain or led away to a dry well.

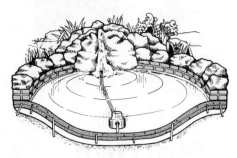

3. Cut the 1 × 2s into 11″ stakes, marking each at 2″, 5″, and 8″ distances from the head. Drive them into the bed at square-foot intervals up to the 8″ mark.

4. Fill the pool with 3″ of sand or gravel as a subbase (up to the 5″ marks).

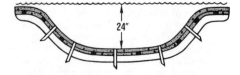

24″

5. Lay the wire mesh into the pool, supporting it about 2″ above the subbase with small stones or brick bits.

6. Pack the prepared concrete mix firmly around the mesh with the shovel up to the 2″ stake marks. This will give you a 3″ concrete basin.

7. After the concrete loses its sheen, finish it with the trowel or wooden float.

8. Cure the concrete for at least 3 to 4 days by covering it with plastic. Drain and refill the pool several times before stocking it with fish or plants.

For Best Results

Vary the depth of the pool to suit your taste, but it should have a minimum center depth of 14″ to keep fish safe from other animals and a 16″ depth for water plants.

A gentle slope makes laying the concrete easier; however, you can make the slopes as steep as you wish. For a steeper slope, mix the concrete with slightly less water than in other construction for convenience in laying it.

For added effect, lay a border of large stones around the lip of the pool and brush a coat of QUIKRETE® Masonry Coating on the basin. It's available in white, gray, and other popular colors.

CONCRETE BLOCK POOL

An uncomplicated design, the concrete block pool has rectangular corners that add a dignified elegance to any garden, and its construction makes it an easy and economical project to do yourself.

SITE EXCAVATION

1. Plan the size of your pool so that no blocks will have to be cut. Since no mortar will be used, use the actual dimensions of the block, which are 1/8″ less than the nominal dimensions.

Tools and Materials

QUIKRETE® Concrete Mix
QUIKWALL® Surface Bonding
  Cement
QUIKRETE® Masonry Coating
QUIKRETE® Hydraulic Water-Stop
  Cement
6" × 8" × 16" concrete blocks
2" × 8" × 16" concrete capping blocks
8" length of 1/2" copper or plastic
  tubing
Reinforcing wire
1" × 2" scrap lumber
Shovel, mason's hammer, trowel, 4'
  level, ball of line, screed, wooden
  float, portable mixer, and brush

2. Stake out an area 1' wider on the sides and ends than the planned external dimensions of the pool.

3. Excavate the site. For a reflecting pool using only one course of blocks, excavate at least 4"; for a fish or plant pond using two block courses, excavate at least 12". For the overflow pipe to work, a minimum of 3" of the pool, including the capping blocks, must be exposed above ground.

4. The bottom 2" of the site are excavated only to the external dimensions of the pool; try to keep these edges straight so that the concrete slab can be poured without a form.

POOL CONSTRUCTION

1. Lay the reinforcing wire into the pool bed.

2. Pour the prepared concrete around the wire to a depth of 2". Use a hook to keep the wire near the center of the slab for maximum strength.

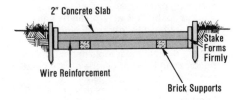

2" Concrete Slab
Stake
Forms
Firmly
Wire Reinforcement
Brick Supports

3. Screed and float the concrete after it loses its sheen.

4. Set the blocks lengthwise into the fresh concrete. Lay them outward from a corner, butting them together as tightly as possible and keeping them aligned with the level. Apply

QUIKRETE® Hydraulic Water-Stop Cement around the bottom of the wall to make it waterproof.

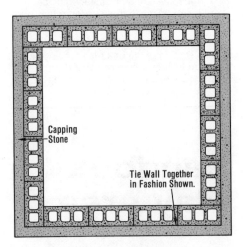

Capping Stone

Tie Wall Together in Fashion Shown.

5. Trowel the prepared QUIKWALL® on both sides and on the top of the blocks, taking care to completely cover them. One 50-pound bag is sufficient to cover an area of approximately 50 square feet to a depth of 1/8". The bed on top of the blocks should be a minimum of 1/4" thick.

6. Lay the capping blocks into the QUIKWALL® bed, overhanging the edges of the wall at least 1" on all sides. Level the blocks in two directions and make certain they are correctly aligned.

7. Insert the tubing as an overflow pipe under the capping blocks in an appropriate location in your wall. Use QUIKRETE® Hydraulic Water-Stop Cement to seal the opening around the pipe. Do this before laying the block.

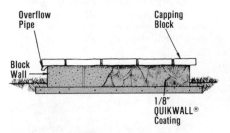

Overflow Pipe
Capping Block
Block Wall
1/8" QUIKWALL® Coating

8. Cure the concrete for at least 3 to 4 days by covering the pool with plastic, then brush a coat of QUIKRETE® Masonry Coating over the entire wall surface.

For Best Results

A drainpipe can be installed in place of the overflow to drain water at the onset of cold weather.

If a drain is not used in your pool, put in a section of log or a piece of firewood in cool weather to absorb the pressure of ice and avoid cracking caused by freeze/thaw cycles.

Sandbox Play Area

Few things exercise a child's imagination like a sandbox, and this project is as easy to build as it is fun to play in. Fill it with QUIKRETE® Play Sand; it's washed, screened, sterilized, and rid of all organic matter before being packaged for sale. And don't forget: It's a good idea to have some means of covering the sandbox to keep out rain, leaves, animals, etc.

Tools and Materials

QUIKRETE® Play Sand
QUIKRETE® All-Purpose Sand
1" × 4" edge boards, 1" × 3" trim boards, 2" × 2" wood and cleats, 5/8" exterior grade plywood, tamper, and bricks

1. Stake out and excavate the play area according to the dimensions shown in the illustration. Border the area with 1" × 4" edging. For details on excavating and edging, see the *Patios, Walkways, and Driveways* section.

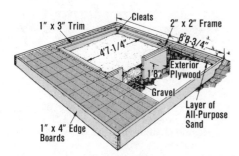

1" x 3" Trim — Cleats — 2" x 2" Frame — 8'8-3/4" — 4'7-1/4" — 1'8" — Exterior Plywood — Gravel — Layer of All-Purpose Sand — 1" x 4" Edge Boards

2. If desired, lay a 1" to 2" gravel base to improve drainage; this is especially important in damp locales.

3. Use 5/8" exterior grade plywood and 2" × 2" wood and cleats to construct the sandbox frame according to the dimensions shown in the illustration. Border the frame with 1" × 3" trim.

4. Fill the sandbox with QUIKRETE® Play Sand.

5. Spread a 1" to 2" layer of QUIK-RETE® All-Purpose Sand over the ground surrounding the sandbox. Tamp the surface smooth, then lay the bricks in rowlock fashion over the entire area.

6. Sweep QUIKRETE® All-Purpose Sand into the cracks between the bricks. After removing any excess sand from the surface, wet it down with a very fine spray; be careful not to allow any pools of water to form.

Patios, Walkways, and Driveways: Brick, Flagstone, Adobe, Stone

Whether the project is a short walkway, a curving drive, or an expansive backyard patio, brick is a surprisingly easy material to use for durability and attractiveness. Depending on the particular project design, most tools and materials needed can be found in the home. Whatever the project, proper drainage requires a slope of not less than 1" per 10 lineal feet. The maximum slope for a driveway is 1-3/4" per foot. Slope away from buildings and toward pavement edges.

SAND BASE

A sand base is an easy method for the beginner and provides good durability in areas not subject to ground-freeze. Two 70-pound bags of QUIKRETE® All-Purpose Sand are enough to cover approximately 144 square feet.

Tools and Materials

QUIKRETE® All-Purpose Sand
Brick paving
Carpenter's level, mason's line or string, rubber mallet/wooden block, screed, and spade

---

CONSTRUCTING THE PAVEMENT

1. Stake out the site and excavate deep enough to allow a 1″ to 2″ sand bed beneath the brick. For good drainage, the brick surface should be kept 1″ above the grade.

2. Edge the site (see *Edging the Pavement,* page 76).

3. Pour QUIKRETE® All-Purpose Sand to a depth of 1″ to 2″; then wet the sand with a fine spray to settle it. Screed level.

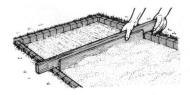

4. Lay bricks outward from a corner, using a mason's line or string to align the rows. Tap and level the bricks in place with a mallet.

5. Sweep QUIKRETE® All-Purpose Sand into the joints; dampen with a fine spray. Resand as needed to fill joints.

For Best Results

Overlay the base with an asphalt-saturated felt or dark polyethylene plastic to prevent weed growth through bricks.

Underlay the base with 1″ to 2″ of gravel or crushed rock to improve drainage in damp locales.

DRY MORTAR

Using dry mortar is almost as easy as using sand and increases the pavement's permanence in areas subject to frost heave. The brick is bonded at the joints, providing a more stable way to construct a driveway.

Tools and Materials

QUIKRETE® Sand Mix
QUIKRETE® All-Purpose Sand
Brick paving
Level, mason's line, rubber mallet/wooden block, 1/2″ wood spacer, burlap sack, and spade

---

CONSTRUCTING THE PAVEMENT

1. Follow steps 1 through 4 as in the sand base method, using a spacer to place the bricks.

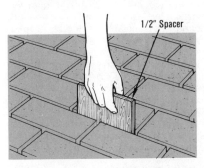

1/2″ Spacer

2. Sweep QUIKRETE® Sand Mix into the joints; use a spacer to tamp the mix for firmer bonding.

3. After removing any excess mix from the paving surface, wet it down with a

very fine spray, taking care not to allow any pools to form or mix to splash out of the joints.

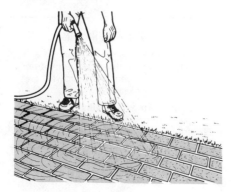

4. Let set for about 2 hours, then scrub the brick face with a wet burlap sack to remove any spillover.

For Best Results

Before spreading the sand mix, make sure brick is dry to avoid staining.

Spray twice to assure sufficient moisture to bond joints.

For a professional look, smooth the joints with a wooden dowel or broom handle after the mix begins to harden.

For a firmer foundation, use QUIKRETE® Sand Mix for the base instead of sand. No additional spraying is needed.

WET MORTAR

In this method the pavers are set in wet mortar over a 4" to 6" concrete slab. This permanent installation method is needed in areas with severe winters or highly unstable soil. If an existing slab is used as the base, repair all cracks and damaged areas with QUIKRETE® Vinyl Concrete Patcher. If the existing slab is painted or extremely smooth, coat it with QUIKRETE® Concrete Bonding Adhesive prior to laying down the mortar bed. This will ensure a strong, lasting bond between the pavers and slab.

LAYING THE BRICK

1. After constructing the header with 1 × 4 lumber against all the open sides of slab, shovel in prepared mortar to a 1/2" depth. Screed only 10 square feet at a time.

Tools and Materials

QUIKRETE® Mortar Mix
QUIKRETE® Vinyl Concrete Patcher
QUIKRETE® Concrete Bonding
  Adhesive
Brick paving and 1 × 4 lumber
Level, mason's line, rubber mallet/
  wooden block, 1/2" wood spacer,
  small masonry trowel, burlap sack,
  flat-edged shovel, and ball peen
  hammer

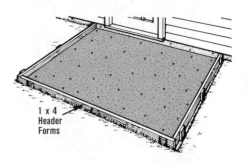

1 x 4
Header
Forms

2. Lay brick outward from a corner, leaving 1/2" joints between the bricks. Use level and line for proper placement, and remember to level in two directions, using mallet/block to place the brick.

3. After letting the brick set in the base for about 4 hours, use a small trowel to carefully work the mortar into the joints. Minimize spillage to avoid staining brick.

4. Let harden 1/2 hour, then finish the joints with a jointer, broom handle, or wooden dowel.

5. Use a wet burlap sack to remove any spillage from brick after about 2 more hours.

For Best Results

To prevent bricks from absorbing too much moisture from the mortar, wet them down several hours before using them.

Mix only enough mortar at one time as you can use in about an hour.

FLAGSTONE, STONE, AND ADOBE

Other paving materials such as flagstone, stone, and adobe can be used instead of brick, depending on the effect desired and the time and expense that can be afforded. Generally, brick is the most versatile for time, design, and economy; but the basic construction techniques and slope requirements are similar for all.

Flagstone is larger and more expensive than brick and is usually laid in an irregular pattern that complements its varying shapes and sizes. It can be cut the same way as brick, if necessary, or it can be purchased precut.

Due to its weight and size, flagstone can be laid directly on an extremely stable, level soil base. In areas where drainage is poor or where traffic is heavy (such as walkways), lay the flagstone on a 3″ or deeper sand base. The dry mortar method can also be used to provide more stability.

For patios and driveways, the wet mortar method is best for setting flagstone. As with all paving, your area's climate will dictate which method is best for any project.

River rock, field stone, and cast concrete pavers are less expensive than flagstone. Sand bed, dry mortar, or wet mortar installation methods can be used. A sand base works well with most concrete paver applications, while the irregular shape and texture of rock and stone make wet mortar the best choice for these materials.

HOMEMADE CONCRETE PAVERS

Precast concrete pavers, often called patio pavers, are available in a wide range of shapes, sizes, and colors. Square, rectangular, or special interlocking designs can be used to create any number of striking patterns. You can also cast concrete pavers using QUIKRETE® Concrete Mix or QUIKRETE® Sand Mix. The simplest method of casting pavers is to dig an earth form in firmly packed soil. Fill the hole with the prepared mix, smooth the surface of the pour, and allow it to cure fully. The paver can then be removed for use. Hinged, reusable wooden forms are also easy to build and

Soil Form for Homemade Pavers

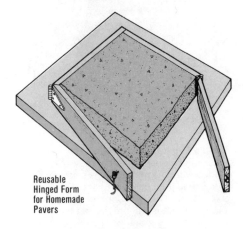

Reusable Hinged Form for Homemade Pavers

use. Trash can lids make excellent forms for round pavers. Place the stone at the bottom of the molds before pouring the concrete. The weight of the poured concrete will do the finishing work for you.

PAVING WITH ADOBE

The simple, economical sand base method is the best way to lay adobe paving. Use 1″ joints between pieces to allow for irregular block sizes and provide proper drainage. To prevent cracking of the finished installation, be sure that the sand base is level and free from stone or gravel.

EDGING THE PAVEMENT

Edging is needed to stabilize the pavement and can most often improve its appeal. Three common methods are shown below.

Soldiers. This is the simplest method. A border of bricks set on end is placed between the pavement site and the surrounding soil. The soil must be firm enough to hold the soldiers in place.

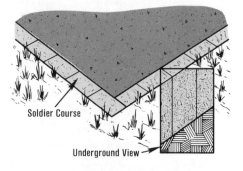

Soldier Course

Underground View

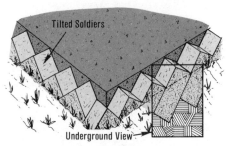

Tilted Soldiers

Underground View

Invisible Edging. As the name indicates, an obvious border can be avoided with this method. It is also more stable than using soldiers. A footer of QUIKRETE® Concrete Mix is poured around the perimeter of the paving site. The footer will be one

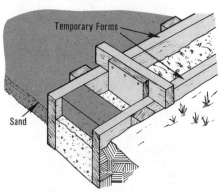

Temporary Forms

Sand

brick length wide and 2″ deep, with the top set one brick width below ground level. After the footer has set, bricks are laid along it in the same method used for the pavement.

Concrete Edging. This is constructed in the same manner as invisible edging, except that the surface of the footer is brought flush with ground level. The face remains exposed and can be finished in a number of attractive ways or simply left smooth.

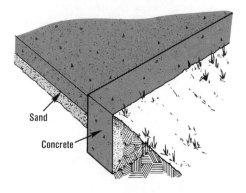

Sand

Concrete

WORKING WITH PAVING MATERIALS

Patterns. The advantage of brick and adobe over stone is that a pattern can be created in the pavement. There are several common methods, or the builder can invent one of his own. The easiest methods for the beginner are those which do not require cutting the paving material. These methods will also reduce waste. Some common patterns, and whether or not cutting is required, are shown here.

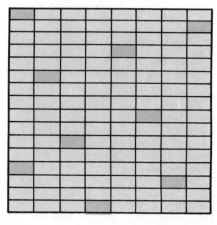

Stack

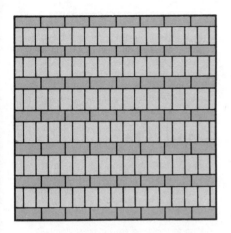

Running Stack

Basket Weave Variation

Running Bond

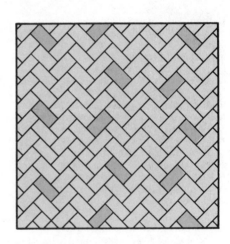

Herringbone

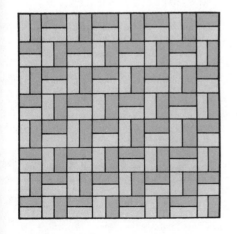

Basket Weave

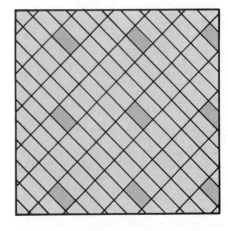

Diagonal

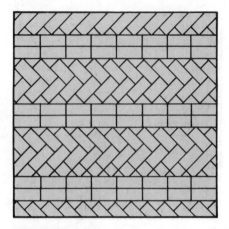

Diagonal Herringbone
Jack on Jack Combination

Cutting. Brick, stone, and adobe are cut similarly. A brick set or broad-bladed cold chisel, mason's hammer, and safety glasses are necessary. The brick is set on a flat surface, and the chisel is placed on the cutline with the bevel facing away from the side to be used. A small groove is cut across all four sides with light hammer taps, and a sharp blow on the broad surface will make the final cut. For larger stones, one end is placed on a solid support, and the unsupported end is tapped to make the final cut. The chisel end of the hammer is used to chip away any rough edges.

Laying the Pavement. Whatever material is used, laying begins at a corner and moves outward. Leveling is done in two directions. Except for brick on a sand base, all paving should have at least 1/2" joints to allow for the mortar fill. Depending on the look desired, the joints should be finished with a trowel or similar object after being filled. To prevent displacing previously laid bricks, a long board should be knelt on while laying the pavement.

Cleaning. Again, depending on the desired effect, you may wish to clean the brick or stone if mortar stains appear. To do this after the mortar has set, soak the area to be cleaned, and then mix a solution of 9 parts water to 1 part muriatic acid. Use rubber gloves to scrub the area, then rinse the area thoroughly to prevent acid burns.

CONCRETE PATIOS

An attractive and durable patio can be made by combining wooden strips with concrete slab construction methods. Redwood is an excellent choice because of its high resistance to rot and decay. Tools and materials are the same as those for concrete slabs (see page 2).

CONSTRUCTION

1. Construct the exterior form. (Refer to page 12 for more information on form construction.) Use the same type of wood that you will use for the strips because the exterior form is not removed after the concrete is placed.

2. Divide the area into boxes, using 2 × 4 lengths of the wood. Notch each piece at the intersections. The patio dimensions should be in multiples of the desired box sizes.

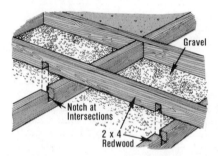

3. Place the cross members on edge and nail them securely into the exterior form frame.

4. Apply a wood sealer/stain before placing the concrete.

5. Mix and place the concrete as described in the section on concrete slabs, page 3. Take care in placing the concrete to avoid having bits of it dry over the strips.

6. When the concrete begins to set, scrub the wood surfaces thoroughly.

Tile Installation

Tile is an extremely versatile surface covering that can be used over floors, walls, ceilings, countertops, shower and bathtub enclosures, and hearths. Used in combination with QUIKRETE® thin-set mixes and grouts, it provides an attractive and durable covering both indoors and out.

Tools and Materials

QUIKRETE® Thin-Set Mix (for setting tile on concrete, exterior-grade plywood, plaster, gypsum wallboard, old tile surfaces, marble, gypsum plaster brown coat, and expanded polystyrene; best for vertical applications)

QUIKRETE® Thin-Set Mix, Sanded (for setting vitreous ceramic mosaics, pavers, and quarry tile on concrete, exterior-grade plywood, portland cement, plaster, gypsum wallboard, old tile surfaces, marble, gypsum plaster brown coat, gypsum block, and expanded polystyrene; best for horizontal applications)

QUIKRETE® Wet Grout (for floor and wall tile that requires presoaking before installation)

QUIKRETE® Dry Grout (for tiles that do not require presoaking before installation; most tiles do not)

QUIKRETE® Acid-Resistant Grout (for joints between glazed and unglazed floor and wall tile, quarry tile, and split brick that is exposed to mild corrosives and abrasive agents)

QUIKRETE® Self-Leveling Floor Resurfacer (for precast floor slabs, new concrete, weather-damaged floor slabs, poured-in-place slabs with unacceptable finishes, and existing floors)

Tiles, spacers, glass cutter, pliers or nippers, notched trowel, chalk line, plumb bob, rubber float or squeegee, toothbrush, sponge, soft cloth, and level

Note: For more information on QUIKRETE® tile-setting products, see pages 123 and 124.

TILING FLOORS

When installing tile over a concrete slab, make sure that the slab is level, properly cured, and free of any dirt, wax, or curing compounds. A smooth, dry slab that has been steel troweled is the ideal base. If it is cracked or damaged in any way, repair it before attempting to

lay the tile. (See *Repairing Concrete* page 96 for details.)

When installing tile over a new wood floor, install a 5/8″ plywood subfloor and put an underlayment of 3/8″ plywood over it. If you're working with an existing floor, remove the finish floor and nail 5/8″ plywood over the subfloor. When installing over old tile, it is a good idea to rough up the surface first for good bonding, then apply QUIKRETE® Self-Leveling Floor Resurfacer to smooth out any worn or rough spots. In all cases, make sure that the base is sound and level before beginning the installation.

SETTING FLOOR TILE

The following method is particularly effective for rooms with large doorways that make the floor visible from other parts of the house.

1. Snap a chalk line down the center of the room perpendicular to the doorway. Now divide the room in quarters by snapping another chalk line perpendicular to the first.

2. Starting at the doorway, dry-lay tiles along the first chalk line. Use scraps of plywood or similar material as spacers between each tile so that the grout spaces will be uniform.

3. If you do not have enough room for a full tile at the end of the line, use a cut tile at each end so that the spaces are equal. To cut a tile, score it with a glass cutter, then lay it over a nail or piece of metal and press down on both sides. Use pliers or nippers to remove any rough edges.

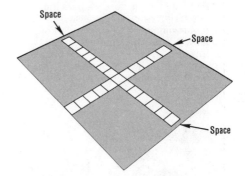

4. Dry-lay tiles along the second chalk line, again using spacers. If necessary, adjust the lines so that they intersect at a tile corner as shown in the illustration.

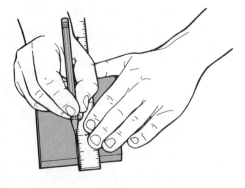

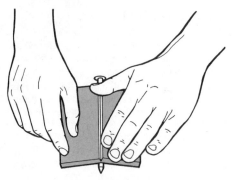

5. Draw a line on the floor to mark the outside edge of the last full tile at the doorway. Make sure the line is straight and extend it along the entire length of the wall. Repeat this procedure on one of the adjacent walls.

6. Place long 1 × 2s or 1 × 3s on the outside of each line. Make sure that they are perfectly square, then nail them in place.

7. Beginning in the corner where the boards intersect, spread a small area (approximately 3 square feet) of mortar with a notched trowel. Hold the trowel at about a 45° angle to achieve maximum coverage. Set the corner tile into the wet mortar with a firm, twisting motion.

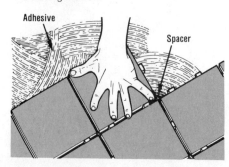

Adhesive

Spacer

8. Continue setting the tiles according to the order shown in the illustration. Always use spacers between the tiles to keep the alignment straight. Use a rubber mallet to tamp down any uneven tiles and wipe all excess mortar off the surface immediately.

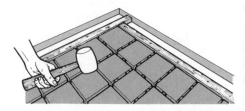

9. When the mortar has set, remove the boards. Lay cut tiles along the edges, leaving an 1/8″ gap along the wall.

GROUTING

Remove the spacers and allow the mortar at least 24 hours to set before grouting. Apply the grout by spreading it diagonally across the tiles with a rubber float or squeegee. Use a toothbrush handle or similar tool to work the grout into the joints. Remove any excess and wipe off the remainder with a wet sponge. Wait until a haze forms on the surface (about 30 minutes), then polish with a soft cloth. Cover the area with plastic sheeting to cure the grout; wait about 72 hours, then apply sealer to the joints to protect the grout from mildew.

Squeegee

Grout

TILING WALLS

If you're tiling over an existing wall, the surface must be free of dirt and wax, and it should be sanded down if it is glossy. If the wall has extensive cracks and other surface defects, install wallboard or some other new backing material over it.

New wallboard must always be sealed with a compatible primer before installing the tile; be sure to cover all cut edges and nailheads completely. Any wet locations, such as shower and bathtub enclosures, require an underlayment of moisture-resistant wallboard or some other waterproof backing.

SETTING WALL TILE

This procedure makes use of a layout rod, a special tool that enables you to simulate a dry run for the wall tile installation.

1. Find the center point of the wall and snap a plumb line from the ceiling to the floor. Snap two more plumb lines close to the edges of the wall.

2. Snap a horizontal chalk line across the exact center of the wall, then snap two more horizontal lines as close to the floor and ceiling as possible. These six lines will provide the centerlines for beginning the tile installation. They also point out where your walls are uneven; in such cases, the tiles must be tapered so that they fit snugly against the wall.

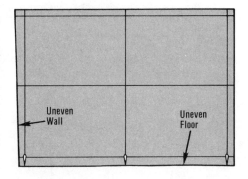

3. To make the layout rods, cut two 1 × 2s to the height and width of the wall. Use a compass to mark a tile

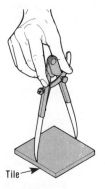

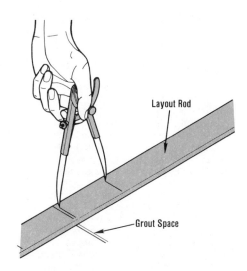

layout along each rod, adjusting the grout spacing and location of the cut tiles until you are satisfied. If you are using special tile or trim pieces as a border, be sure to include them on the proper ends of the rods.

4. To transfer the marks from the rods to the wall, hold each rod against two of the plumb lines or horizontal lines.

5. Begin installing tile on the bottom row, starting at the centerline. Apply enough mortar for the first few tiles, but leave the baseline and centerline visible for accurate alignment.

6. Set the first tiles in place, being sure to insert spacers between them. (For a thinner grout line, use toothpicks or a similar item for the spacers.)

7. Continue setting the tiles, working your way up the wall. Use a level to ensure accurate alignment and squareness.

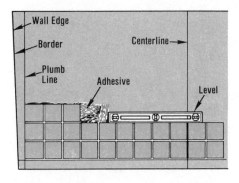

8. Grout the tile in the manner described earlier. If you are grouting in a shower

or bathtub enclosure, be sure to plug the drain to keep grout out of the plumbing. Keep the grout damp for at least 72 hours to allow for proper curing.

TILING COUNTERTOPS

Because a countertop is subject to a good deal of moisture, impact, and other abuse, it is important that high-quality tile is used. It is wise to install glazed tile around sinks and food preparation areas because unglazed tile tends to stain. If you are installing the tile on a plywood countertop, cut slots in the plywood 2" apart to allow for expansion.

Various trim tile pieces are available for the tricky areas of a countertop, including the edges, corners, backsplash, and sink opening. They include surface bullnose, drip-edge bullnose, cove, and quarter-round pieces. For the neatest and most attractive look, a countertop should be covered only with whole tiles. However, since this is not always possible, you might want to install a self-rimming sink instead of mounting the sink below the tile; the rim does a nice job of covering the cut edges.

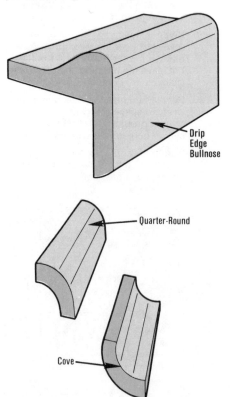

Drip Edge Bullnose

Quarter-Round

Cove

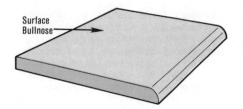

Surface Bullnose

SETTING COUNTERTOP TILE

While tiling a countertop involves a good deal of careful planning, it is not as difficult as many people believe. Use the following procedure:

1. Starting with trim pieces or bullnose tiles and continuing with full tiles, make a dry run of the entire sink. If the counter is L-shaped, start the run at the inside corner and work outward both ways. Use a full tile for the corner piece; all trim pieces should be laid out with the grout lines following those of the rest of the tiles.

2. When the front and back edges are in position, make a dry run of the tiles around the sink. If the sink is self-rimming, lay the tiles in place and mark the cutlines from underneath. If the sink has a recessed basin, cut the tiles and trim the pieces to fit around it.

3. Mark and cut tiles for faucet holes and any other openings as shown in the illustration.

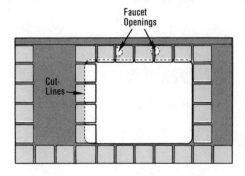

Faucet Openings

Cut-Lines

4. When you are satisfied with the entire layout, mark the tiles and/or the countertop with the necessary cut marks. Do *all* cutting before beginning tile installation.

5. The procedures for cutting, setting, and grouting countertop tile are identical to those outlined earlier. To prevent mildew, apply a good sealer about two weeks after the installation.

Mortarless Block Construction with QUIKWALL®

QUIKWALL® Surface Bonding Cement now makes most block construction possible without using mortar; it's literally a "stack and stucco" project. A single coat on dry-stacked block gives a handsome stucco finish and provides greater flexural and impact strength than mortar with less expense. A 50-pound bag will cover approximately 50 square feet. In planning your project, note that actual rather than nominal block size is used since joints are not buttered.

BLOCK WALLS

The same basic techniques of wall construction are used no matter what your project happens to be.

Tools and Materials

QUIKWALL® Surface Bonding Cement
QUIKRETE® Concrete Repair or QUIKRETE® Concrete Mix, depending on the project
Mason's line, level, concrete or joint trowels, and chalk line
Mason's hammer, brick set, straightedge, metal tie bars, and metal lathe strips

---

CONSTRUCTION

1. Construct the footer for the wall. (Refer to *Footers for Walls*, page 9.)

2. To ensure square, accurate corners and straight walls, dry-lay the corner

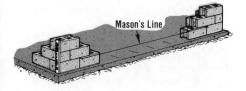

Mason's Line

leads and first course and chalk mark the block positions on the footer. Use a level and mason's line for accuracy.

3. Remove the blocks and lay 1/8" bed of prepared QUIKWALL® on the footer. Re-lay the bottom course, checking alignment and level every 3 to 4 blocks.

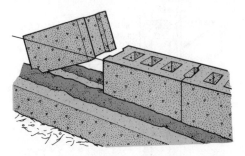

4. For projects with wall openings or intersecting walls (other than at corners), refer to steps 6 and 7. Otherwise, dry-stack the remaining block in a running bond pattern to the desired height, checking every few courses to maintain proper height. If necessary, shim with QUIKRETE® All-Purpose Sand or Sand Mix.

5. Wet down the wall and apply 1/8" QUIKWALL® coat to both the sides and exposed ends of wall using a finishing trowel with an upward motion.

6. Stack and bond the main and bearing wall intersection together in 4- to 6-course intervals. After the main wall has been stacked and coated no higher than 6 courses, begin constructing the intersecting wall. It too

should be placed in an 1/8″ bed of QUIKWALL®. Embed metal ties every 4 to 6 courses as shown. Stuffing the bottom of the block cell opening with paper will allow you to fill it with mortar to hold the tie. Continue to build the intersection in intervals to the full height of the wall.

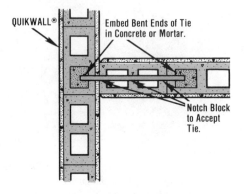

QUIKWALL®

Embed Bent Ends of Tie in Concrete or Mortar.

Notch Block to Accept Tie.

7. To construct window or door openings, dry-stack the block no more than 2 or 3 courses higher than the bottom of the opening before framing out the opening to exact dimensions. The wall is then built up around the frame. Precast lintels make finishing the top of doors and windows easy. Simply lay in place and coat with QUIKWALL®.

8. Control joints to handle stress and prevent cracking should be located approximately every 20′ in the wall. They are also required at the following points of weakness and/or high stress concentration:

- At all abrupt changes in wall height
- At all changes in wall thickness, such as those at pipe or duct chases and those adjacent to columns or pilasters
- Above joints in foundations and floors
- Below joints in roofs and floors that bear on the wall
- At a distance of not over half the allowable joint spacing from bonded intersections or corners
- At one or both sides of all door and window openings unless other crack control measures are used, i.e., joint reinforcement or bond beams

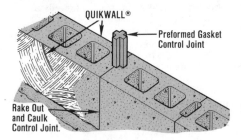

QUIKWALL®

Preformed Gasket Control Joint

Rake Out and Caulk Control Joint.

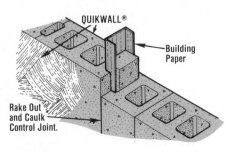

QUIKWALL®

Building Paper

Rake Out and Caulk Control Joint.

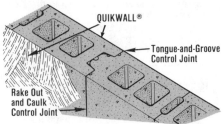

QUIKWALL®

Tongue-and-Groove Control Joint

Rake Out and Caulk Control Joint

Regardless of the control joint design used, rake out the wall joint and caulk with QUIKRETE® Concrete Repair Caulk.

9. Attach capping sills to the top course by anchoring bolts firmly into the concrete or QUIKWALL®. Moist-cure the wall after 8 hours by dampening

with a fine spray. Repeat several times daily for 3 days. Roof or floor construction can proceed when the curing is complete.

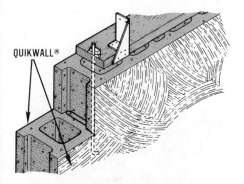

QUIKWALL®

For Best Results

Take extra care that the bottom course is laid properly, because each succeeding course will simply be stacked on it.

To ensure proper bonding, make certain that the blocks are clean and free of any dirt, soil, or grease.

Before laying the block, remove any burrs and chips from it with a hammer to get a tight fit.

Mix only as much QUIKWALL® as can be used in 1 hour.

To obtain the finish you desire, experiment with different trowels and techniques before applying the QUIK-WALL® coat to your wall.

Gallery of Mortarless Block Projects

Take a look at some of the things you can build using the technique of mortarless block construction.

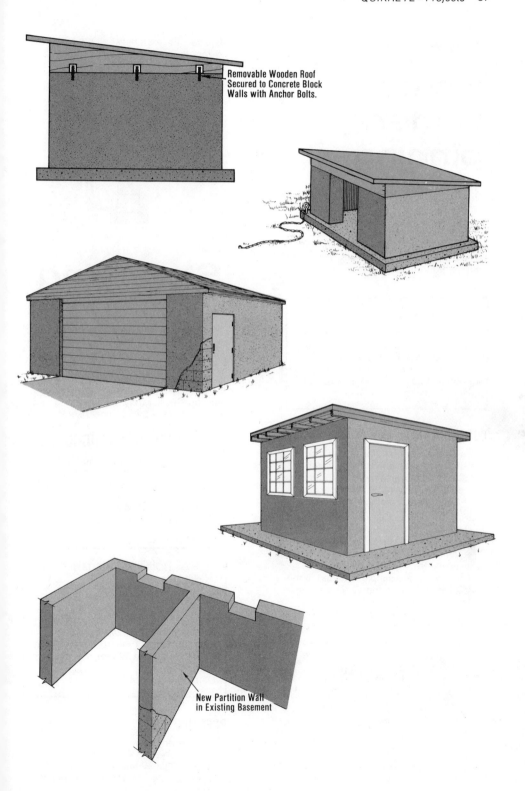

Removable Wooden Roof
Secured to Concrete Block
Walls with Anchor Bolts.

New Partition Wall
in Existing Basement

Mobile Home Under-pinning

QUIKRETE® mortarless block construction is an ideal method of finishing off mobile home installations. When building up underpinning, plan the work so that the top course of block rests flush with the bottom of the mobile home.

Tools and Materials

See those listed under *Footers for Walls* (page 9) and *Mortarless Block Construction with QUIKWALL®* (page 83).
In addition, you will need sufficient amounts of vent block, drip cap, and quality caulking.

CONSTRUCTION

1. Use a plumb bob to locate the exact front of the wall and then construct a suitable footer (see page 9). Build up the wall as you would any other type of QUIKWALL® installation (see page 83).

2. Mobile home underpinnings require ventilation. Special foundation vents equal in size to concrete block are available from building suppliers. These vents are simply included in the stacking pattern during construction. They should be placed in one of the middle courses every 10 to 12 blocks depending on local building codes.

3. Slope the final grade away from the home to prevent water from collecting against the block.

4. Caulk the joint between the home and top course of block and install a drip cap to prevent water penetration

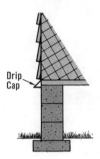

Drip Cap

Stuccoing

Stucco is an attractive and durable cement-based coating frequently applied to masonry and wooden structures. It is usually white, but it can be colored by adding mineral pigments during the mixing process. Stucco can also be painted, although it will rarely need painting. It is also unaffected by rust and insects.

APPLYING STUCCO

Stucco is usually applied in three coats: scratch coat, brown coat, and finish coat. Use QUIKRETE® Mortar Mix for the first two coats. A two-coat method is occasionally used on masonry and concrete construction in hot, dry climates.

Tools and Materials

QUIKRETE® Mortar Mix
QUIKRETE® Stucco Finish
Mixing box, mason's hoe, hawk, trowel, float, plaster rake, masonry brush, and wire brush
Hammer, nails, 15-lb. roofing felt, and expanded metal lath for nonmasonry surfaces
Caulking gun and caulk

PREPARATION

1. On wooden structures, nail the roofing felt over the area to be stuccoed. The felt is attached in vertical strips with a 3″ overlap. Use galvanized nails.

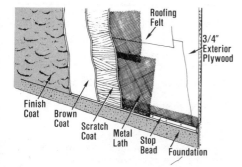

Finish Coat
Brown Coat
Scratch Coat
Metal Lath
Stop Bead
Foundation
Roofing Felt
3/4" Exterior Plywood

2. Nail the steel mesh over the paper with galvanized nails. Do *not* use aluminum nails; they react chemically with the cement in the mortar mix.

3. Scrub new masonry surfaces with a wire brush and water for a clean bond. If the surface is very smooth, apply a coat of QUIKRETE® Bonding Adhesive.

APPLYING THE SCRATCH COAT

1. Using enough water to achieve a putty-like consistency, prepare as much mortar as can be used in about an hour.

2. Trowel the mortar onto the surface from bottom to top on concrete or masonry surfaces, and from top to bottom on wire mesh. Make certain that concrete and masonry surfaces are damp before applying the mortar.

3. The scratch coat should be about 1/2" thick. Force it through the wire mesh on wooden structures so that it is about 1/4" thick behind the mesh.

4. Smooth the scratch coat with the trowel.

5. After the coat has set enough to be firm but not hard, use the rake to scratch horizontal grooves about 1/8" deep across the face of the mortar.

APPLYING THE BROWN COAT

1. Apply the brown coat when the scratch coat is strong enough to bear the weight. This will usually be about 4 to 5 hours—sooner in hot, dry, and windy weather and later in cold weather. With open-frame wood construction, do not apply the brown coat for at least 48 hours after applying the scratch coat.

2. Dampen the scratch coat; prepare as much mortar mix as can be used in an hour.

3. Apply the brown coat to a thickness of about 3/8" using the float and hawk.

4. Screed the brown coat evenly as shown. After it loses its sheen, float it smooth.

5. Moist-cure the brown coat by dampening it with a fine spray of water every few hours for 2 days. Air-cure it for 5 more days.

APPLYING THE FINISH COAT

1. Trowel on a 1/8"-thick coat of prepared stucco finish, starting at the bottom and working to the top.

2. Depending on the desired texture and finish, the coat can be applied evenly or unevenly. You can give an even texture distinctive finishes by lining it using a broom, slapping it with a leafy branch or the mason's brush, or by flinging small gobs onto it and floating them almost flush with the smooth layer. Several finishes are shown here.

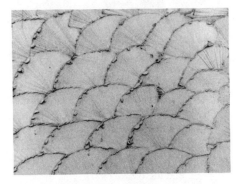

3. Moist-cure the finish coat for 5 days by misting it periodically with a fine spray.

4. Seal all the joints around doors and windows with a masonry-compatible caulk.

For Best Results

Apply the brown coat and finish coat to an entire wall at a time to avoid coloration differences.

If the brown coat will not be applied to the scratch coat within 4 or 5 hours, mist the scratch coat periodically.

While applying stucco, do not try to get tight joints around windows and doors. The caulk will take care of sealing the joints.

Do not rake the scratch coat so hard that stucco is removed. Only rake hard enough to score the coat. A piece of lath or a wooden block with nails driven into it will also do a good job of raking.

After the finish coat has been applied, wait a day before moist-curing it.

Do not apply stucco to a frozen surface or when freezing temperatures are likely.

Insulating Foundation Walls

If your house has uninsulated concrete basement walls, you can reduce heat loss substantially by installing rigid insulation covered with QUIKWALL® Fiberglass Reinforced Foundation Coating. Panels can be made of extruded polysty-

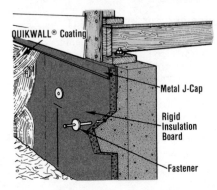

rene foam (blue board), expanded polystyrene (white bead board), urethane panels, pressed glass fiberboard, or other rigid insulation materials. It is best to insulate to the frost line, but substantial savings are possible even if insulation is applied from the bottom of the siding to a depth of 1' below grade.

Tools and Materials

QUIKWALL® Fiberglass Reinforced Foundation Coating
Rigid insulation panels, fiberglass tape, fasteners and washers, medium-heavy paintbrush, acrylic latex or silicone caulk, caulking gun, metal J-channel capping, hammer, shovel, straightedge, tape measure, saw or utility knife, and trowel

---

WALL PREPARATION

Determine the depth to which you are going to insulate. One foot below grade should be your minimum. To estimate the amount of rigid board needed, measure from the bottom edge of the siding to the below-grade depth and multiply by the perimeter of the house. This will give you the square footage of board needed. To prepare for installation do the following:

1. Dig out the soil from the foundation to the required depth.
2. Apply a bead of caulking to the underside of the bottom edge of the siding.
3. Nail or fasten the metal J-channel to the foundation, pressing the channel into the caulk to prevent water from flowing behind the channel and insulation. Fasten the channel beneath the edge of all siding and around all door and window openings.

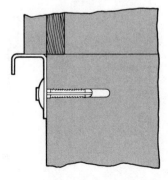

INSTALLING THE INSULATION

The rigid board can be secured to the foundation with special concrete fasteners and washers or with panel and foam adhesives specially formulated for use with rigid insulation board.

1. Measure and cut the insulation panel to size using a saw or utility knife. (With certain types of extruded polystyrene boards, the clear plastic coating must be removed prior to installation.) Make certain all panels butt tightly against one another and the J-channel.

2. If securing with fasteners and washers, predrill the proper size holes through the rigid board into the foundation on 24" centers both vertically and horizontally. Holes must be deep enough to accommodate the fasteners and allow the washers to be recessed into the panel. Butt the panels at the corners so one panel overlaps the other.

3. If securing with an adhesive, use only those adhesives designed to be used with rigid foam insulation. Solvent-based construction adhesives will destroy the installation board. Apply the adhesive according to the manufacturer's instructions.

4. Apply self-sticking fiberglass tape to the joints between the insulation panels, to all outside corners, and over all fastener heads and damaged panel areas. Brush dirt and residue from the insulation surface.

5. Mask around channels, windows, and doors to prevent contact with the masonry coating.

APPLYING THE COATING

1. Mix the QUIKWALL® Fiberglass Reinforced Foundation Coating according

to package directions. You might want to slightly increase the amount of water added to set a more "brushable" consistency. If the mix begins to stiffen during work, remix, and add small amounts of water as needed.

2. Use the trowel to precoat all taped areas with QUIKWALL® mix.

3. With a brush or trowel, cover the insulation panels to the desired thickness. To prevent color variation, cover the entire wall corner-to-corner in one work session. Clean the brush or trowel periodically to avoid a buildup of coating.

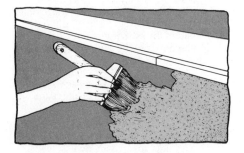

4. The final coating thickness should be approximately 1/8", although a thicker coating can be applied if the surface must withstand abuse. The final coat is best applied with a stiff-bristled brush.

FINISHING

1. Remove all masking tape.

2. Replace the dirt from around the foundation, sloping it so that water runs away from the foundation.

3. Caulk around channels, doors, and windows to prevent moisture from penetrating behind the coating.

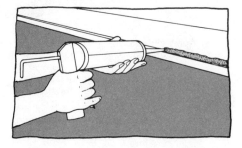

4. If desired, the coated panels can be painted with QUIKRETE® Masonry Coating (see page 129 for further details).

Property Markers

When Mason and Dixon placed their survey markers along the Pennsylvania-Maryland border in 1767, they were clearly identifiable as well as accurate. A boundary dispute is one of the most vexing situations that can confront a property owner, and many disputes are the result of survey features having changed over the years, pins that have been partially covered or buried by overgrown weeds, or stakes that have been removed because they were not recognized as survey marks.

Cast concrete markers that are 4" × 4" are solid, durable, noticeable and, because they are clearly identifiable as markers, unlikely to be accidentally removed.

Tools and Materials

QUIKRETE® Concrete Mix
1/2" plywood (32" × 10" per form)
Oil or concrete release agent
Wire

MARKERS

1. Cut the plywood into eight sections with the following dimensions: 5" × 10" (2); 4" × 10" (2); 4" × 6" (2); and 3" × 6" (2).

2. Center the 3" × 6" pieces on the 5" × 10"s and the 4" × 6" pieces on the 4" × 10"s. Glue or tack the pieces together to make sides for the form.

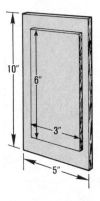

Side

3. Coat the interiors with a thin film of oil or a release agent.

4. Fit the sides together and bind them at the top and bottom with the wire.

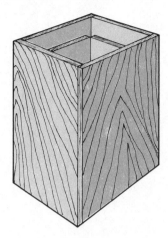

5. Fill the form with the prepared concrete mix; poke a stick, broom handle, or similar object into the form to compact the concrete and remove any air pockets. Screed the concrete flush with the form.

6. Allow the concrete to cure for at least a day before removing the form.

For Best Results

After the concrete has received its initial set, customize the marker cap with the date of installation, survey, and the owners' names.

Well Collars

When installing a well, the casing must extend above the ground at least 6″ (preferably a full foot) in order to keep out ground water. A concrete well collar placed around the protruding end of the casing provides drainage as well as an effective, watertight seal. Simply pour QUIKRETE® Concrete Mix in a 2′ radius around the casing. Use a trowel to slope it away from the casing as shown in the illustration. For best results, the collar should be poured 4″ thick.

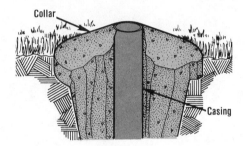

SECTION II: REPAIR AND MAINTENANCE WITH QUIKRETE®

While it is true that masonry is one of the most long-lasting and durable types of construction, some form of maintenance and/or repair work will eventually be needed. In this section, you'll learn how to deal with routine repairs, such as surface cracks and flaking concrete, as well as more involved procedures like tuck-pointing mortar joints and repairing sunken brick. We've also included helpful tips designed to save you time and money. And remember, QUIKRETE® has a full line of masonry repair products on hand to help you get the job done as quickly and as easily as possible.

Repairing Concrete

Flaking, chipped, or cracked concrete is not only unsightly, it can also lead to further deterioration of the concrete. Many concrete repairs can be made simply and quickly at little cost with QUIKRETE® concrete repair products. Taking the time now to do the repairs will be well worth the effort.

MINOR CRACKS AND FLAKING IN CONCRETE SURFACES

Minor flaws such as small cracks or flaking are so easily repaired with QUIK-RETE® Vinyl Concrete Patcher and QUIKRETE® Concrete Repair Caulk that it takes almost more effort to avoid the repairs than it takes to do them. Vinyl concrete patcher in a 40-pound bag is enough to resurface 20 square feet, 1/4" thick, under average conditions.

Tools and Materials

QUIKRETE® Vinyl Concrete Patcher
  or QUIKRETE® Concrete Repair
  Caulk
QUIKRETE® Concrete and Asphalt
  Cleaner
Wire brush, brush, and small trowel or
  caulking gun

REPAIRS

1. Vigorously rub the wire brush against the crack or flaking area and remove any cracked or crumbling concrete.

The tip of the trowel is used to pry up loose sections of the flaked concrete.

2. Use the brush to remove loose particles and dust.

3. Clean the area with the concrete and asphalt cleaner. Rinse with clean water. Do not leave any surface water.

4. Prepare as much QUIKRETE® Vinyl Concrete Patcher as can be used in a half hour. Let it sit for 10 minutes, then restir it *without* adding any more water.

For better adhesion add QUIKRETE® Concrete Acrylic fortifier to the water before mixing the patcher.

5. Apply the mix with a trowel and taper the edges smooth with the surrounding concrete (called featheredging).

6. For narrow cracks, simply caulk them
with QUIKRETE® Concrete Repair
Caulk after brushing away dust and
loose particles.

For Best Results

Apply the vinyl concrete patcher in
layers a thickness of 1/4" or less. If
more than one layer is needed for the
repairs, allow several days curing time
between layers.

Because vinyl concrete patcher is a
stiff mix, you must keep the trowel
wet and clean while applying the mix
so it does not curl up on the trowel.
Do not add more water to the mix.

Use concrete repair to caulk the many
areas around the house, barn, or storage shed where concrete and masonry surfaces should meet with framing
members. Be sure that the gaps are
filled so that the material overlaps the
edges of the opening.

WIDE OR DEEP CRACKS AND HOLES

For cracks shallower than 1-1/2" to 2",
the vinyl concrete patcher can be used
for repairs. For cracks deeper than 2",
use QUIKRETE® Sand Mix and QUIK-
RETE® Concrete Bonding Adhesive. Ten
80-pound bags of sand mix and 1-1/2
quarts of concrete bonding adhesive are
sufficient to cover a 40 square foot area
that is 2" thick.

Tools and Materials

QUIKRETE® Vinyl Concrete Patcher
or QUIKRETE® Sand Mix and
QUIKRETE® Concrete Bonding
Adhesive
QUIKRETE® Concrete and Asphalt
Cleaner
Cold chisel, ball peen hammer, or 8-
pound sledgehammer
Safety glasses or goggles, gloves,
brush, broom, square trowel, and
pointing trowel

REPAIRS

1. Undercut the edges of the crack at
least 1" below the concrete surface
with the chisel and hammer. Brush
out all loose concrete, dust, and other
foreign materials until there is a solid
base for the repairs.

2. Wet the repair surface and lightly
scrub it with concrete and asphalt
cleaner. If there is grease or oil on the
exposed concrete subsurface, let the
cleaner soak for 5 minutes before
rinsing off the concrete. If necessary,
repeat until the repair surface is clean.

3. If the crack is small enough to apply
vinyl concrete patcher, trowel the
material into the crack in quarter layers and allow several days curing time
between layers.

4. Featheredge the final layer smooth with the surrounding concrete surface.

5. For cracks requiring the application of sand mix, brush or roll well-stirred concrete bonding adhesive onto the exposed subsurface as thick as a coat of paint.

6. After the adhesive coat becomes tacky, place the prepared sand mix over the entire repair surface. Immediately level and smooth with the trowel.

7. After all surface water has evaporated and the concrete has lost its sheen, smooth and compact it with overlapping passes with the trowel.

For Best Results

Keep the trowel pressed firmly and flat into the sand mix when finishing the concrete.

Use a wooden float for finishing to give the concrete a textured, nonskid finish.

CRACKS AND HOLES IN WALLS

The steps for repairing holes and cracks in concrete walls are the same as those to repair holes and cracks in walks, driveways, floors, and so forth. The tools and materials are the same as the ones required for repairing wide or deep cracks and holes.

REPAIRS

1. Undercut the edges of the hole or crack with the chisel and hammer.

2. Thoroughly clean all loose dirt and particles of concrete from the undercut area. Scrub out the opening with concrete and asphalt cleaner so a firm bond will be made.

3. Apply the concrete bonding adhesive as you would a thick coat of paint.

4. After the adhesive becomes tacky, tightly pack premixed sand mix or vinyl concrete patcher into the opening with a pointing trowel.

5. Immediately trowel the area smooth and flat with the surrounding concrete surface.

6. When the surface loses its sheen, smooth and compact the concrete with the trowel using firm, overlapping passes. Hold the trowel flat.

For Best Results

Allow the concrete to cure for several days before doing any more work in the patch area. Keep the patch covered with a sheet of plastic to help curing.

For corner repairs, use an edger with a 1/2″ radius to round the edges.

Repairing Steps

Tools and Materials

QUIKRETE® Quick-Setting Cement or QUIKRETE® Sand Mix
QUIKRETE® Concrete Bonding Adhesive
QUIKRETE® Concrete and Asphalt Cleaner
Cold chisel, ball peen hammer, goggles and gloves, pointing trowel, plasterer's trowel, and paintbrush
Scrap lumber (for wood forms)

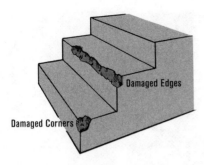

Damage on concrete steps usually occurs at the leading edges of the tread or at corners. To repair broken steps

1. Undercut and widen the broken area with a cold chisel and hammer. Remove all dirt and loose concrete and clean the surface with concrete and asphalt cleaner.

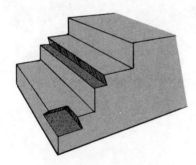

2. Use QUIKRETE® Quick-Setting Cement as directed on the package to build up the surface to the desired height after applying a coat of concrete bonding adhesive. A pointing trowel works well for most applications.

3. Finish and smooth the edges and corners flush with the adjoining step surfaces using a square trowel.

For Best Results

Keep the trowel clean and wet while applying the mix.

Use forms for larger repairs or when the stair tread projects out from the riser.

Use QUIKRETE® Sand Mix and QUIKRETE® Concrete Bonding Adhesive as directed on page 100 if buildup is greater than 2".

Do not attempt to finish or shape the edges or corners until the concrete has been in place long enough to retain a firm thumbprint.

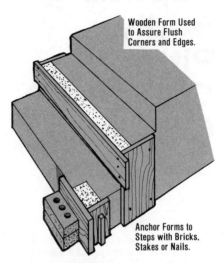

Wooden Form Used to Assure Flush Corners and Edges.

Anchor Forms to Steps with Bricks, Stakes or Nails.

Include Wood Molding in the Forms for more Decorative, Protruding Stair Treads.

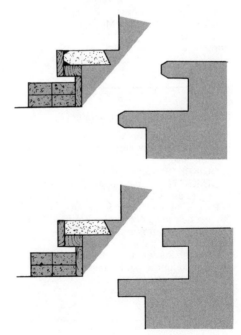

QUIKRETE® Quick-Setting Cement sets hard in 5 to 10 minutes. For formless repairs in which concrete application is expected to take more than 5 minutes, use QUIKRETE® Vinyl Concrete Patcher.

Repairing Badly Pitted/ Chipped Concrete Surfaces

2. Remove all broken and loose concrete, dirt, dust, and plant remains to form a sound base for the new topping.

Use QUIKRETE® Sand Mix and QUIKRETE® Concrete Bonding Adhesive to resurface damaged concrete to depths up to 2". Ten 80-pound bags of mix and 1-1/2 quarts of adhesive are enough to cap an area of 40 square feet 2" thick.

For depths greater than 2", use QUIKRETE® Concrete Mix to build up the damaged area and then cap with a 2" topping coat of Sand Mix.

3. Set and stake forms against the old sidewalk or slab. Backfill against the forms to ensure sufficient support.

Tools and Materials

QUIKRETE® Sand Mix
QUIKRETE® Concrete Bonding
  Adhesive
QUIKRETE® Acrylic Fortifier
QUIKRETE® Concrete Mix (for pouring to depths over 2")
Pickax, shovel, hammer or half-hatchet, saw, level, finishing trowel, bricklayer's trowel, edger, broom, cold chisel, ball peen hammer, sledgehammer, and safety goggles
Forming lumber and stakes
Wheelbarrow
Curing materials

SITE PREPARATION

1. Dig a small trench along the edge of the damaged surface so that forms can be set in place level with the old concrete surface.

4. Use a level to make sure that the forms are set at the correct height and that there is adequate slope for drainage.

MAKING THE REPAIR

1. Apply QUIKRETE® Concrete Bonding Adhesive to the prepared surface as you would a thick coat of paint. Wait until the adhesive becomes tacky before pouring concrete or sand mix.

2. For deeper repairs, mix a sufficient amount of QUIKRETE® Concrete Mix, and fill in the low spots, especially along form edges.

3. Mix QUIKRETE® Sand Mix with water until a plastic-like consistency is obtained.

4. Add QUIKRETE® Acrylic Fortifier to the sand mix as part of the liquid component, not separately from or in addition to water. Blend thoroughly.

5. Trowel the sand mix onto the damaged area.

6. The sand mix layer should be no greater than 2" thick.

7. Trowel the surface smooth using a steel finishing trowel. Edge using a concrete edger if desired.

8. To assure a nonskid surface apply a broom finish. Always pull the broom toward you, use light pressure, and do not overlap the strokes.

9. Cure the new topping as you would a new concrete installation.

For Best Results

Avoid using patching material during extremely hot or cold weather.

Break up badly broken concrete with a sledgehammer and make a new pour. Use some of the broken pieces of the old concrete to take up space in the new pour. Install steel reinforcement rods where extra support is needed.

Follow the general finishing tips given in the projects section *Concrete Sidewalks and Small Slabs.*

Repairing Concrete Walks

Over a number of years, even correctly placed concrete sidewalks can be badly damaged and cracked by impacts, severe freeze/thaw cycles, and grade changes caused by such things as tree growth. Minor problems can be corrected by using the methods discussed in *Repairing Concrete* (page 96). For more serious damage, follow the steps below, which are similar to those previously described.

Tools and Materials

QUIKRETE® Concrete Mix or
 QUIKRETE® Sand Mix
QUIKRETE® Concrete Bonding
 Adhesive
QUIKRETE® Concrete and Asphalt
 Cleaner
Sledgehammer or pick, shovel, and
 brush
Mixing box and hoe

REPAIRS

1. Break up the area to be repaired with a sledgehammer or pick. If the problem is a pavement section that has been uplifted by tree roots and cannot be simply relaid, break enough concrete off the corner to make a large notch to permit releveling of the section.

2. Relevel the gravel base if it has sunk; use the broken concrete as filler.

3. Brush the edges of the remaining concrete and wash with concrete and asphalt cleaner to remove any organic refuse that might interfere with the repair's bond.

4. Apply the concrete bonding adhesive to all exposed edges of the old concrete. Erect temporary forms along the edges.

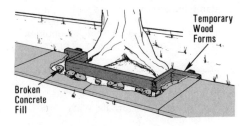

Temporary Wood Forms

Broken Concrete Fill

5. Place the concrete and cure for 3 to 4 days. For more information on curing and finishing the concrete, refer to page 36.

For Best Results

Reinforcing can be added before placing the new concrete. Drill holes in the exposed concrete edges and insert large bolts into them; use QUIKRETE® Anchoring Cement to bond them to the concrete. Fasten wire mesh to the bolts and place the concrete.

Where a notch has been cut out around a tree trunk, sink a border of treated 2 × 4s flush with the grade. They can also be used as forms for placing the concrete.

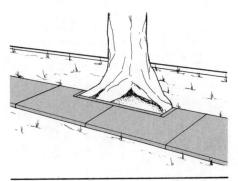

Repairing Leaks in Concrete and Masonry

Despite the best construction methods, any concrete construction can eventually develop cracks through which moisture can leak, leading to further deterioration of the structure. If the cracks are in a water-holding vessel, such as a swimming pool, cistern, or fountain, they might not only be unsightly and a source of deterioration, they can also interfere with the efficiency or use of the structure. Follow these simple steps now to avoid drastic measures later.

Tools and Materials

QUIKRETE® Hydraulic Water-Stop Cement
Pail, wooden paddle, and trowel
Hammer, chisel, wire brush, scraper, and hose

REPAIRING THE LEAKS

1. If the cracks are in a water-holding vessel, drain the water or wait until it is at a low enough level for the repairs to be done safely.

2. With a hammer and chisel, enlarge all cracks and holes. Cut squarely or undercut; do not enlarge the cavities by making tapered, V-shaped cuts. The cavities should be enlarged to at least 3/4" deep and 3/4" wide.

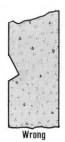  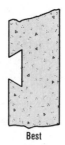

| Wrong | Good | Best |

3. Remove all loose material from the cavities, then scrub them out with a wire brush and water.

4. With a pail, a wooden paddle, and water, prepare only as much QUIKRETE® Hydraulic Water-Stop Cement as you can apply in a 3-minute period. Roll the mixed amount in your hands until you feel it begin to stiffen and become warm.

5. Beginning at the top, press the cement into the cavity with your fingers. Maintain pressure for a few minutes or until the cement sets and the leak stops.

6. Smooth the surface with water and a trowel. Keep the area moist for at least 15 minutes. When all cracks and holes have been repaired, coat the entire wall with QUIKRETE® Masonry Coating.

Repairing Wet and Leaking Basement Walls

Damp basement walls can be caused by either condensation on the inside or water penetrating through the wall from the outside. To see if condensation is the problem, tape a 1'-square piece of aluminum foil to the wall with all four sides of the foil airtight. Keep the foil on the wall for 2 days, then remove and examine it. If the outside of the foil is moist, the problem is condensation. This can be corrected by installing a dehumidifier or by increasing the ventilation in the basement. If, on the other hand, the foil that was facing the wall is wet, the problem is water penetration.

One or two coats of QUIKRETE® Masonry Coating is ideal for waterproofing damp basement walls. However, if the walls are actually leaking, QUIKRETE® Hydraulic Water-Stop Cement should be used first to fill the cracks and holes.

Tools and Materials

QUIKRETE® Hydraulic Water-Stop Cement
QUIKRETE® Masonry Coating
Pail, wooden paddle, and trowel
Hammer, chisel, wire brush, scraper, and hose

LOCATING AND REPAIRING LEAKS

1. Check your house to find the source of the leak. Sources include downspout gutters and soffits. If the source cannot be shut off or redirected, plug the leak.

2. Follow the steps given in the preceding section for repairing leaks in concrete and masonry. When all holes and cracks have been repaired, coat the entire base of the wall with QUIKRETE® Masonry Coating.

Water-proofing Concrete and Masonry

Whether new or old, concrete structures should be treated to prevent the entry of deteriorative moisture. It's easy to do—if you can paint you can waterproof—and well worth the effort.

Tools and Materials

QUIKRETE® Masonry Coating
QUIKRETE® Hydraulic Water-Stop Cement
Large mixing vessel, heavy-duty masonry brush, wooden paddle, wire, brush, scraper, and hose

WATERPROOFING

1. If the surface is new, scrub it with a wire brush and rinse it with water. If the surface is especially smooth (poured concrete, for example) etch the surface with a 20% to 25% solution of muriatic acid, then rinse.

2. If the masonry surface is old or if it has been covered with paint or some other coating, it must be cleaned thoroughly before applying the QUIKRETE® Masonry Coating. Remove all loose mortar, dirt, and paint with a wire brush or scraper; **at least 75%** of the original masonry surface should be exposed. Scrub it with a wire brush and rinse thoroughly.

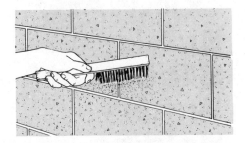

3. Any cracks, holes, and visible leaks should be filled at this time with QUIKRETE® Hydraulic Water-Stop Cement as described in the preceding sections. Allow the patched areas several days for curing before going any further.

4. Mix the masonry coating in a mortar box; for smaller jobs, a pail or similar container will do. Dampen the entire wall before applying.

5. With a heavy-duty masonry brush or a coarse-fiber calcimine brush, apply the paint to the wall. Use a circular scrubbing motion to ensure good penetration. Allow 24 to 48 hours drying time before dampening the wall again and applying a second coat.

For Best Results

Apply a bead of water-stop cement around the basement wall where it meets the floor.

Add mix to the water; don't add water to the mix.

Restoring with QUIKWALL®: Buildings, Silos, and Water-Holding Tanks

QUIKWALL® Surface Bonding Cement adds strength, durability, and water resistance to concrete block, brick, stone, concrete, and any other structurally sound wall. It's ideal for restoring buildings, silos, chimneys, cisterns, and other water-holding devices. Use it combined with QUIKRETE® Concrete Acrylic Fortifier when greater adhesion and/or water resistance is required.

Tools and Materials

QUIKWALL® Surface Bonding Cement
QUIKRETE® Concrete Acrylic Fortifier (as needed)
QUIKRETE® Hydraulic Water-Stop Cement (as needed)
QUIKRETE® Masonry Coating (as needed)
Trowel
Chicken wire, hammer and nails, and sandblasting equipment (as needed)

BUILDINGS

QUIKWALL® is very effective in restoring older buildings whose walls have begun to crack and loosen from the effects of time. An 1/8" coating of QUIKWALL® on the outside of walls makes them practically impermeable to cold air drafts, so it's particularly suited for use on horse barns and other farm buildings.

1. Clean and dry all walls thoroughly. It is important that the walls be free of paint, oil, dirt, and other foreign matter that can interfere with good bonding.

2. If you are working with concrete block or some other good bonding surface, the QUIKWALL® can be applied directly to the wall. Apply an 1/8"-thick coat using a finishing trowel with an upward motion.

3. If you are working with plywood, expanded polystyrene foam, or some other surface with poor adhesion, nail chicken wire over the entire wall; this will provide a good mechanical bond for the QUIKWALL®. Mix the QUIKWALL® with QUIKRETE® Concrete Acrylic Fortifier and apply the mix directly over the wire.

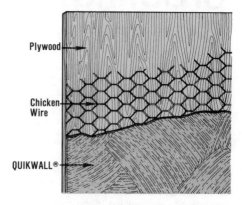

Plywood

Chicken-Wire

QUIKWALL®

4. Moist-cure the walls after 8 hours by dampening them with a fine spray. Repeat several times daily for 3 days.

CISTERNS, HOLDING PONDS, AND OTHER WATER-HOLDING TANKS

Because QUIKWALL® is highly water-resistant, it can be used as a lining on cisterns, holding ponds, and other water-holding tanks to prevent water loss. It is approved for use with potable water, so it's perfectly safe for both humans and animals. Be sure the surface is completely clean and dry before beginning the application, then apply the QUIKWALL® as described earlier. When the QUIKWALL® has completely dried, brush on a coat of QUIKRETE® Masonry Coating.

Note: If large cracks exist on the walls of the structure, it is recommended to first patch them with QUIKRETE® Hydraulic Water-Stop Cement. (For details, see

Repairing Leaks in Concrete and Masonry section page 103.) When the cement has dried completely, begin applying QUIKWALL® over the entire surface.

SILOS

QUIKWALL® provides the best protection against the acid that commonly forms in silos. Keep in mind that for the QUIKWALL® to bond well surface preparation is especially important in this application.

1. Sandblast the interior walls of the silo to remove the accumulated acid crust.

2. Remove the remaining traces of acid by washing the walls with lime water, then go over them again with plain water. Allow them to dry completely before beginning the QUIKWALL® application.

3. Apply the QUIKWALL® in the same manner as described earlier. When relining silos, it is very important that the walls be troweled extra smooth to minimize the occurrence of small pockets where future acid attack could originate.

CHIMNEYS

Without a doubt, chimneys must withstand a great deal of abuse from the elements. And while tuck-pointing repairs helps restore them to good condition, the improvement is only temporary. To do a job that will last, coat the entire part of the chimney that extends above the roof with an 1/8″ coating of QUIKWALL®. Its high strength and water-resistant properties are ideal for combating wind, rain, ice, and snow.

Repairing with Quick- Setting Cement

Many homeowners neglect repairs to precast pieces, chipped concrete statuary, and even angled concrete (such as steps and corners) out of a lack of confidence in their abilities to work with concrete, or a feeling that the repairs are not worth the effort of making suitable forms. QUIKRETE® Quick-Setting Cement makes these and similar jobs simple enough for even the inexperienced do-it-yourselfer to achieve more than satisfactory results. Specially formulated for use where rapid setting and high strengths are needed, it sets in 5 to 10 minutes and can be sculpted with a trowel to match the surrounding surface without any lengthy delays. No forms are needed. It just might take more patience and know-how to bring in a Georgia catfish.

Tools and Materials

QUIKRETE® Quick-Setting Cement
Pointing trowel or bricklayer's trowel
Hammer, chisel, safety glasses, and brush

REPAIRS

1. Undercut and/or square the edges of the damaged area with a hammer and

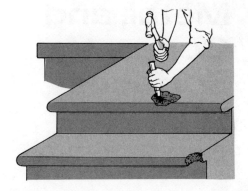

chisel. Be sure to wear safety glasses to prevent injury from flying chips of concrete.

2. Brush all loose material and dirt from the area to be repaired. Dampen the damaged surface.

3. Apply the cement to the damaged surface, rough-shaping it to the proper contours as it is applied. Prepare only as much cement as can be applied in about 5 minutes.

4. After the concrete receives its initial set (several minutes), sculpt it to its finished form by shaving it with the edge of the trowel.

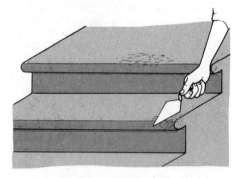

For Best Results

Use QUIKRETE® Concrete and Asphalt Cleaner to wash the damaged surface for a more certain bond.

Skidproofing Wood, Metal, and Concrete Surfaces

Combine QUIKRETE® Sand Mix and Concrete Acrylic Fortifier to create a nonskid surface around pools, walks, and boat docks.

Tools and Materials

QUIKRETE® Sand Mix
QUIKRETE® Concrete Acrylic Fortifier
Masking tape, trowel, brush or broom, hoe, and mixing box

APPLICATION

1. Lay masking tape around the edges of the surface to be coated. Make certain that the surface is clean and free of dust, dirt, and loose matter.

2. Mix 1-2/3 quarts of fortifier with 60 pounds of sand mix; for larger and smaller mixtures refer to the directions on the back of the fortifier bottle. Add water to achieve the desired consistency.

3. Trowel the mix onto the surface in a 1/16"- to 1/4"-thick coat.

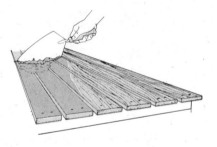

4. Brush the mix to achieve a rough texture.

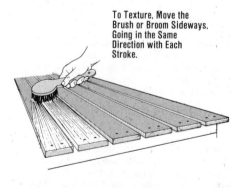

To Texture, Move the Brush or Broom Sideways, Going in the Same Direction with Each Stroke.

For Best Results

Acrylic paint can be added to the wet mix before application if a particular color is desired.

Sealing Around Pipes

The cutout openings around basement pipes are prime areas for moisture to enter your home, not to mention insects and vermin. To keep these unwelcome visitors out of your home, seal around all pipes with QUIKRETE® Quick-Setting Cement. It's specially formulated so that you can sculpt it to fit securely around pipes for an effective, watertight seal.

Tools and Materials

QUIKRETE® Quick-Setting Cement
Hammer and chisel or keyhole saw
   and mason's trowel

SEALING

1. Square the edges of the hole with a hammer and chisel.

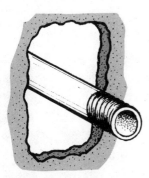

2. Be sure the edges of the hole are free of dirt and other loose material, then dampen the area slightly.

3. Mix the QUIKRETE® Quick-Setting Cement just long enough to obtain a smooth, lump-free consistency. Make the initial application with a mason's trowel, filling in the hole generously.

4. After the initial set, work the patch with the edge of the trowel to firm up the concrete around the pipe.

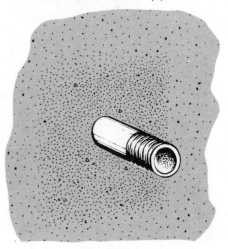

Note: If your basement is warm and dry, it is best to keep the patch moist for 24 hours by covering it with polyethylene film.

Repairing Damaged Trees

QUIKRETE® Sand Mix is ideal for sealing small cavities in trees. This procedure is especially helpful in preventing the spread of insects and diseases that lead to tree decay.

1. Brush out the cavity thoroughly to remove all the deadwood and other loose material.

2. Coat the surface of the cavity with a pruning compound.

3. Drive several large nails into the cavity; they will help hold the concrete while it sets.

4. Fill the cavity slightly beyond the growing layer of bark with QUIKRETE® Sand Mix.

Tuck-Pointing Mortar Joints/ Replacing Damaged Brick

The cutting out and repointing of mortar joints in brick, block, and stone masonry is one of the most common repairs performed by masons. Left unrepaired, water can seep in between the cracked, loose mortar and cause interior wall damage.

Tools and Materials

QUIKRETE® Mortar Mix, or QUIKRETE® Vinyl Concrete Patcher, or QUIKRETE® Hydraulic Water-Stop Cement
Plugging or joint chisel, bricklayer's hammer, wire brush or bristle brush, garden hose, jointer, pointing trowel, and wheelbarrow or mortarboard

---

MIXING THE MORTAR

While QUIKRETE® Mortar Mix is the product of choice for most applications, especially larger jobs, other QUIKRETE® products also give excellent repointing results. If you plan to make a number of concrete repairs such as filling cracks, repairing chipped edges, resurfacing scaled areas, as well as doing some repointing, QUIKRETE® Vinyl Concrete Patcher can handle all these jobs. And if you plan to patch leaks in block or brick walls with QUIKRETE® Hydraulic Water-Stop Cement, repoint the surrounding joints as well. Always follow the directions listed on the individual product package.

When using QUIKRETE® Mortar Mix for repointing, it is recommended that you prehydrate the mortar prior to tuckpointing joints. This step will greatly reduce the shrinkage of any of the joints away from the edge of the bricks and cut down on the number of hairline cracks that occur when the mortar begins to dry against the old bricks.

To prehydrate the mortar, mix the required amount of QUIKRETE® Mortar Mix with just enough water to form a damp unworkable mix that retains its form when pressed into a ball in the hand. Let the mortar set for about 30 to 45 minutes, and then add enough water to make the mortar workable. The end result will be a mix slightly drier than that normally used to lay new brick. Never make large batches of mortar for repointing; mix an amount you can use in about 45 minutes.

PREPARING THE JOINTS

1. Cut out the mortar joints to an approximate depth of 3/4" to 1". Use of the special plugging or joint chisel will help prevent binding in the joint and chipping of the brick edges.

2. A clean surface is needed for good bonding. Use the jointer tool to rake out excess mortar or grit, and brush out the joints to remove loose mortar or sand.

3. Flush out any remaining particles with a garden hose equipped with a spray attachment.

REPLACING BAD BRICKS

Any bricks in the wall that are badly broken or deteriorated should be cut out and replaced prior to repointing. Select new bricks that match the old bricks as closely as possible.

1. Cut the old brick completely out of the wall.

2. Clean out the recess carefully.

3. Wet the cavity and the replacement unit with a brush or fine spray of water. When the cavity is damp, but not wet, apply a thick layer of QUIKRETE® mortar to the bottom and sides of the cavity.

4. Butter the top of the replacement brick and slide it into the cavity. Mortar should squeeze out from the joints. If it does not, rebutter the joint, adding more mortar.

REPOINTING

1. Dampen the cleaned joints with a brush and water.

2. Load the trowel with mortar. Pick up the mortar from the trowel with the jointer tools and press it into the joints. Pack the mortar firmly into the joints. Repoint the head joints first and the bed joints second. This sequence allows you to make unbroken horizontal strokes with the jointer to form straight, even bed joints.

3. In most cases, joints are filled flush to the wall face, then slightly depressed with the jointer and brushed clean. If concave or V joints were used in the original work, strike with the proper tool for these finishes after the repointing is done and before the mortar gets too hard to work.

4. To decrease the possibility of cracking or sagging in extremely deep joints, fill in about half of the joint depth, wait until the mortar is thumbprint hard, and then repoint the remainder of the joint.

5. In hot or windy conditions, dampen the repointed joints to prevent the mortar from drying too fast. Spray the finished job with a fine water mist to aid in the curing process.

6. Repointing of stonework and block is essentially the same as brickwork. Tool the joints to match those in the sound sections of the wall.

Repairing Chimneys

Although repairing a leaning chimney or one that is leaking smoke through the brick joints are jobs best left to a professional, there are some important repairs that anyone can perform. These include repairs to preserve the integrity of the brickwork and to avoid more serious and expensive work in the future. If your chimney has crumbling pointing or holes and cracks in the cap, doing the repairs yourself immediately will prevent further weakening and avoid the costly job of rebuilding or replacing it later. Getting up to the chimney might require some time and effort because scaffolding is usually necessary, but the repairs themselves are straightforward tasks.

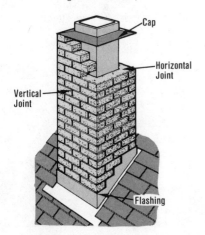

REPOINTING A CHIMNEY

Repointing a chimney does not require a great deal of mortar. QUIKRETE® Mortar Mix is available in bags conveniently sized to provide just enough mortar for the present job or to have a little left over for other small jobs. QUIKRETE® Vinyl Concrete Patcher can be used instead for better adhesion.

Tools and Materials

QUIKRETE® Mortar Mix or QUIKRETE® Vinyl Concrete Patcher
Mason's 2-lb. hammer, 3/8" chisel, brush, brick trowel, and mortarboard
Scaffolding, heavy gloves, and safety glasses or goggles

CLEANING AND REPOINTING

1. Hold the chisel at a sharp angle to the joint while striking it with a hammer and knock out the crumbling joints to a depth of at least 1/2". Work the chisel along the joint about 1" at a time.

2. Chip out vertical joints first, then do horizontal joints.

3. Brush any loose particles of dirt or mortar out of the joints.

4. Dampen the joints.

5. Prepare as much mortar as can be used in 1 hour and trowel it into the vertical joints first, then the horizontal joints. Strike the joints flat.

6. After the mortar hardens, brush off any excess.

7. In the course of repointing, you might come across a loose brick or two that should be replaced. Use the chisel to remove the mortar from around the loose brick, then lift it out. Scrape all loose or crumbling mortar from the hole.

8. After cleaning the brick of any mortar and dirt, dampen the brick as well as those surrounding the cavity. Butter its top, bottom, and both ends and press it back into the opening. Make sure the joints are completely filled and strike them flat.

For Best Results

When working on or around any part of a chimney, be sure to close all dampers leading into it so if any soot is knocked loose it will not enter the house.

REPAIRING THE CAP

1. Brush out any loose particles, dirt, and organic matter from cracks and holes in the cap.

2. Dampen the crack or hole and trowel in fresh mortar to fill it flush with the surrounding surface.

3. The cap should be replaced only if it is badly cracked or if the mortar is so loose that it is pulling away from the brickwork. Use the hammer and chisel to chip the cap away in pieces. For safety, lower the pieces in a bucket instead of just letting them fly off the roof.

4. Brush away all dirt and loose particles.

5. Trowel on the fresh mortar in several thick layers, sloping the cap down from the flue liner to the outside edges of the chimney stack.

For Best Results

When working on the chimney, close all dampers to prevent any soot knocked loose from entering the house.

Use safety glasses or goggles and gloves if the repairs are going to require extensive concrete chipping. Eye injuries and scaffolding work can be a very dangerous combination.

FLASHING REPAIR

Chimney flashing should be inspected if there are interior water stains in the area of the chimney. If the flashing is loose, simple repointing is needed; if the flashing has deteriorated, it will have to be replaced.

Tools and Materials

QUIKRETE® Mortar Mix
Joint raker, brush, pointing trowel, and slicker jointer

REPOINTING FLASHING

1. Rake out loose and crumbling mortar from the joints where the flashing and chimney stack meet.

2. Brush any loose particles and dust out of the joint.

3. Dampen the interior of the joint and any remaining mortar. Pack fresh mortar into the joint with the pointing trowel.

4. After the mortar has set slightly, strike the joint flat with the slicker.

For Best Results

If both vertical and horizontal joints have to be repointed around the flashing, repoint the vertical joints first.

Repairing Sunken Brick or Stone Walks/ Patios

Repairing stone or brick paving that has sunk is a task even the novice do-it-yourselfer can perform to restore both safety and attractiveness. But before beginning, try to determine the cause of the damage and remove it to avoid repeating your efforts. If water erosion has undermined the base (such as from a gutter downspout), first try removing the source or redirecting the flow. Installing a bed of gravel or a concrete base beneath the pavement and setting the pavers in a wet mortar mixture will also increase the permanence of the repairs. For more information on paving bases, refer to *Patios, Walkways, and Driveways* (page 72).

MORTARLESS PAVING

If the cause of the sinking is only ground settlement over the years, these repairs can most likely be done with only nominal expenditures of time, effort, and money. If the cause is more serious, a different paving method might be called for.

Tools and Materials

QUIKRETE® All-Purpose Sand Mix
Carpenter's level or a straight length of 2 × 4
Shovel and broom

REPAIRS

1. Remove any loose, broken, or sunken pavers. If your examination shows that adjacent pavers have not been displaced, but that settlement has occurred beneath them as well—so that they are not sitting squarely on the base—they should also be removed.

2. Fill the depression with QUIKRETE® All-Purpose Sand up to the level of the surrounding base.

3. Set the pavers back into place. Check their level with the surrounding pavement with the carpenter's level or 2 × 4. If the pavers are not level, tap them gently to seat them. Replace any broken pavers.

4. Spread all-purpose sand over the repaired area and sweep it into the joints. Dampen the sand with a fine spray; repeat until the joints are completely filled.

For Best Results

For greater strength, dry QUIKRETE® Mortar Mix can be substituted for the joint sand. Follow the same repair procedures.

MORTARED PAVING

Mortared joints and a concrete base make sinking infrequent in mortared paving, but when it does occur it usually indicates a more serious problem than just ground settlement. Before making the repairs after the sunken pavers are removed, check and correct any problems with area drainage.

Tools and Materials

QUIKRETE® Mortar Mix
QUIKRETE® Sand Mix or Concrete Mix (if necessary)
QUIKRETE® Concrete Bonding Adhesive (if necessary)
Mason's hammer, joint chisel or cold chisel, trowel, jointer, hoe, hawk, and mixing box
Shovel, sledgehammer, float, and wire mesh reinforcing (if necessary)

REPAIRS

1. With the hammer and chisel remove the pavers in the sunken area. Do this as carefully as possible to avoid breaking the pavers.

2. Examine the slab base for breakage. If there is major damage, that section of the slab should be removed with the sledgehammer and replaced with fresh concrete. Before placing the new concrete, track down and correct the cause of the problem. For more details on placing the new concrete, refer to *Repairing Concrete Walks* (page 102). If the cause of the sinkage cannot be corrected, use the wire mesh to reinforce the concrete.

3. If the damage or sinking of the slab is relatively minor, use sand mix to bring the area back to the level of the surrounding concrete. Be sure to clean the original slab of any dirt, dust, soil, and organic matter before placing the sand mix. After it is placed, float it and allow it to cure for 3 to 4 days before replacing the paving.

REPLACING PAVING

1. Chip all the old mortar from the pavers with the hammer and chisel. Brush the bed and head joints clean of any loose flakes or dust.

2. Lay in a 1/2″ mortar bed on the concrete slab.

3. Begin laying the pavers from an outside corner of the damaged area using the same size joints as in the original paving. Butter the head joints of each paver before placing it. Replace any broken pavers.

4. Strike the tops of the joints flat to prevent water entry. After the mortar is dry enough to be brushed without smearing, brush away any loose particles of mortar.

For Best Results

Clean all surfaces to be bonded with QUIKRETE® Concrete and Asphalt Cleaner before applying the concrete or mortar mixes.

Repairing Blacktop

Repairs to blacktop, asphalt, or macadam driveways, tennis and basketball courts, and similar constructions are repairs you can easily do yourself with QUIKRETE® products, whether the problem is a slight crack or a more troublesome chuckhole.

CHUCKHOLE PATCHING

QUIKRETE® Blacktop Patch is designed and manufactured to be used to repair even large chuckholes with a firm and durable patch without mixing or heating. Use it just as it comes in the bag.

Tools and Materials

QUIKRETE® Blacktop Patch
Chisel or handpick, small broom or
   brush, and tamper

PATCHING THE HOLE

1. Chisel the edges of the hole straight down to a depth of at least 2"; square off the hole as much as possible.

2. Sweep all loose material out of the hole.

3. Pour in the blacktop patch to a thickness of 2". Tamp solid.

4. For holes deeper than 2", continue building up the patch in 2" increments until there is a slight mound of patch above the surface of the driveway. Tamp solid after each one; after the final one, tamp the patch level with the driveway surface.

For Best Results

Keep the blacktop patch in a warm location until it is ready to be used. Do not use it if the temperature is below 50° F.

Sprinkle dry sand or cement on the surface of the patch to speed curing and to remove the adhesiveness of the patch's surface.

Do not use the patch when rain is expected within a few hours.

Allow the patch to cure for 1-1/2 days before driving over it.

Wait 5 days before applying any sealer.

CRACK REPAIRS

QUIKRETE® Driveway Crack Filler is available in sizes from a 1-quart bottle to a 55-gallon drum to make repairs as easy as possible. One gallon will cover 20 lineal feet of cracks 1/2" deep and 2" wide.

Tools and Materials

QUIKRETE® Driveway Crack Filler
QUIKRETE® All-Purpose Sand (as
   needed)

REPAIRING THE CRACK

1. Remove all loose dirt, soil, and organic matter from the crack.

2. Pour the filler into the crack to within 1/8″ of the surface.

3. For deep cracks, sprinkle clean sand into the crack to within 1/2″ of the surface before applying the crack filler.

For Best Results

Apply the filler only when the outside air temperature is above 50° F.

Before applying the filler, shake or stir it to be sure it is well mixed.

QUIKRETE® Blacktop Repair Caulk is also ideal for repairing cracks in driveways.

Repairing Stucco

One of stucco's advantages as siding is that it rarely needs repairs, and when it does need repairs they are usually simple. However, if the area to be repaired is more than 2 square feet, the stucco should be removed all the way down to the wall surface and built up as described in the preceding section. For more common repairs, including cracks, read on.

Tools and Materials

QUIKRETE® Stucco Finish
QUIKRETE® Concrete Acrylic Fortifier
Hammer, cold chisel, knife, wire brush, and trowel

REPAIRS

1. Remove loose stucco from the damaged area.

2. Use the hammer and chisel or knife to undercut the stucco surrounding the damaged area so that the patch will be locked in.

3. Use the wire brush to remove any stucco knocked loose in undercutting. Brush the entire damaged area free of dirt, dust, and other foreign materials.

4. Thoroughly wet down the damaged area and keep it damp for 12 hours before patching to prevent the moisture from being drawn too quickly from the patch and weakening it.

5. Mix QUIKRETE® Stucco Finish with QUIKRETE® Concrete Acrylic Fortifier. Tightly pack the prepared stucco finish into the damaged area with a trowel and texture it to match the surrounding stucco.

6. For deep repairs extending to the scratch coat, first tightly pack the hole within 1/4" of the surface. Keep the patch damp for 2 days while it sets.

7. Dampen the edges of the hole and the surface of the first layer; trowel in a second layer level with the original stucco and texture it to match.

Regrouting and Replacing Tile

REGROUTING TILE

As grout gets older, it tends to chip away. This allows water to seep behind the tile and, eventually, it will loosen. When regrouting is necessary, proceed as follows:

1. With a putty knife, dig out the old grout. Remove all loose material, then dampen the joint.

Tools and Materials

QUIKRETE® Thin-Set Mix
QUIKRETE® Thin-Set Mix (Sanded)
QUIKRETE® Wet Grout
QUIKRETE® Dry Grout
QUIKRETE® Acid-Resistant Grout
QUIKRETE® Self-Leveling Floor Resurfacer
Putty knife, toothbrush, hammer, straight bar or chisel, trowel, and plastic sheet

Note: The type of mix and grout you'll need to do the repair depends on the specific application. For the various uses of QUIKRETE® mixes and grouts, refer to the *Tile-Setting Products* section on page 128.

2. Apply the new grout, working it into the joints with a toothbrush.

3. Smooth the grout with your finger. Be sure to clean off any excess from the tile immediately.

REPLACING TILE

In those cases where the grout is beyond repair, your only choice is to replace the tile. Use the following technique:

1. If only a few random tiles must be replaced, use a hammer to break them up. Remove all the pieces of tile and grout.

2. If you are replacing an entire section of tile, use a hammer and a straight bar or chisel to loosen the top tile. It should work free by tapping lightly with the hammer. Work down and remove the rest of the tile in the same manner.

3. Once the old tile has been removed, use the putty knife to completely remove the old adhesive. On larger areas, it is a good idea to sand the entire surface with a belt sander after scraping with the knife.

4. Apply the mortar and set the new tile. (See the *Tile Installation* section on page 78 for details.)

5. Wait a day or two for the mortar to set, then remove the spacers, dampen the joints, and apply the grout.

For Best Results

If you are working in a shower or bathtub enclosure, protect the tub by covering it with a sheet of plastic to prevent tile chips from scratching it.

When working around fixtures with a hammer and straight bar or chisel, be careful to avoid damaging the fixtures.

Repairing Drywall and Plaster

Holes and cracks in plaster and drywall are easily repairable. QUIKRETE® Patching Plaster in 5-pound and 25-pound bags makes the job even easier with its slow setting time, allowing more plaster to be mixed and worked at one time and a virtually no-shrinkage formula.

Tools and Materials

QUIKRETE® Patching Plaster
Broad-edged putty knife, pocketknife
or file, brush, plasterer's trowel (for
larger repairs), and a sanding block

PATCHING CRACKS

1. Undercut the edges of each crack
   with the tang end of your file or
   pocketknife so that the inside opening is wider than the face.

2. Brush out the loose particles and
   dust.

3. Thoroughly dampen the edges using
   a brush or plant sprayer.

4. Use cross-hatched strokes with the
   putty knife to fill all voids in the crack
   with patching plaster.

5. After filling each crack, immediately
   remove excess plaster from the wall.

6. After the patch has dried for several
   hours, sand it smooth with a fine-
   grade sandpaper.

For Best Results

Patching plaster should be applied in
several layers for especially wide or
deep cracks. Allow several hours drying time between layers.

Place a primer paint coat on the patch
if it is to be painted.

PATCHING HOLES

1. Undercut around the edge of each
   hole with a sturdy knife or other sharp
   tool.

2. Chip away loose fragments.

3. Brush loose particles and dust from
   hole; thoroughly dampen backing and
   edge.

4. For holes in drywall without backing
   or that go all the way through plaster,
   insert a piece of wire mesh with a
   piece of wire run through it.

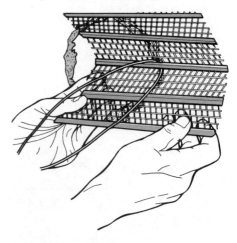

5. Tighten the wire around a pencil or
   similar object until the mesh is held
   firmly against the wall.

6. Use the putty knife to smooth the
   plaster into the hole, about halfway to
   the surface. If a wire mesh is being
   used, leave an opening for the pencil
   wire so that it can be removed after
   the plaster hardens.

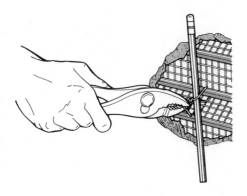

7. Rewet the first coat after it has hardened. Smooth on the second coat to a
   level just below the surface.

8. Rewet the second coat after hardening. Use plasterer's trowel to achieve a
   smooth finish on the final coat; press
   heavily on the trowel to pack the final
   coat tightly.

9. After the final coat stiffens slightly,
   rewet the surface with a clean brush.
   Immediately retrowel, tipping the
   leading edge up slightly, while pressing heavily on the trailing edge, to
   produce a shiny finish.

For Best Results

For smaller holes without backing—
where a lighting fixture is removed,
for example—rolled up paper can be
used to fill the hole as a backer for the
plaster instead of wire mesh.

SECTION III: MATERIALS, TOOLS, AND PLANNING WITH QUIKRETE®

As you've seen in the previous sections, concrete, brick, block, stone, tile, and other masonry products provide the beauty, durability, and versatility no other building material can match. When problems occur, repairs can be made with a minimum of time and effort. Anyone who can plan and work carefully using the basic tools and techniques discussed in this section can complete any of the projects and repairs illustrated earlier. This section introduces you to all of the QUIKRETE® products, a quality line that will take the guesswork and much of the labor out of masonry work.

QUIKRETE® cement mixes.

QUIKRETE® PRODUCT LINE

The QUIKRETE® line of masonry construction and repair products includes everything you'll need to successfully build and repair with concrete. The following product descriptions are intended as a guide to help you select the best QUIKRETE® product for your particular job.

QUIKRETE® Cement Mixes

One of the most problematic aspects of standard concrete and masonry work has always been selecting the proper ingredients and mixing them in correct proportions. Finding quality, clean, organic-free aggregates at convenient locations is sometimes difficult, and transporting, handling, and storing materials can be bothersome and expensive, especially for smaller jobs.

QUIKRETE® ready-to-use mixes solve the problem of correct proportioning and simplify your material selection, transportation, and storage problems. Every bag contains the correct blend of cement and clean aggregate for concrete or mortar. Just add water and mix as directed, and you're ready to begin work. Conveniently sized bags let you buy just the amount you need, so there's no concern about what to do with that little extra sand or gravel piles that's often left when mixing from scratch. You're handling one product, not two or three. And with QUIKRETE®, quality is assured.

QUIKRETE® Concrete Mix. Concrete mix is used for any type of general concrete work, such as building sidewalks, steps, patios, driveways, curbs, footers, floors, post settings, and slabs. Uniform aggregate size makes mixing, placing, and finishing easier. A 60-pound bag covers approximately a half cubic foot; see page 152 for further information regarding yield.

QUIKRETE® Sand Mix (Fine Topping). This all-purpose mixture of cement and fine sand is designed for jobs where concrete is needed in less than a 2″ thickness. Sand mix cures to a stronger finish than ordinary concrete because of its higher cement content. It can also be used for filling cracks, resurfacing, stuccoing, grouting drain tile, and laying flagstone and paving bricks. A 60-pound bag covers approximately a half cubic foot; see page 152 for further information regarding yield.

QUIKRETE® Mortar Mix (Masonry). This mix simplifies mixing mortar for laying brick, block, or stone. A blend of masonry-type cement and graded sands, QUIKRETE® Mortar Mix can also be used for repairing and tuck-pointing existing masonry walls and surfaces. A 60-pound bag covers approximately a half cubic foot; see page 153 for further information regarding yield.

QUIKRETE® Concrete Repair and Resurfacing Products

There's a QUIKRETE® product for virtually every type of concrete repair.

QUIKRETE® Vinyl Concrete Patcher. A blend of vinyl resins, very fine sand, and portland cement, QUIKRETE® Vinyl Concrete Patcher is a truly versatile product. Just add water to mix a completely self-bonding material that is suitable for use both indoors and outdoors. Use it to patch cracks in foundations, walks, slabs, and stucco. Vinyl patcher is also excellent as a "tuck-pointing mortar" and is easily shaped to repair chipped edges on steps, ledges, and cast concrete. This product is also an exceptional resurfacing material for use on driveways, patios, and other concrete surfaces. It is as durable and tough as acrylics, and can be featheredged to 1/16″ thickness. A 40-pound bag will repair an area of approximately 20 square feet to a 1/4″ depth.

QUIKRETE® Quick-Setting Cement. This mix is specially formulated to set hard in only 5 to 10 minutes. Use it for making repairs where high strength and rapid setting are needed such as on damaged swimming pools, septic tanks,

QUIKRETE® concrete repair and resurfacing products.

retaining walls, precast concrete pipe, well covers, culverts, curbing, and other concrete units such as birdbaths, sundials, etc. This cement can be sculpted during application and retempered when necessary. A 7-pound pail will cover approximately 100 cubic inches.

QUIKRETE® Anchoring Cement. QUIKRETE® Anchoring Cement expands as it hardens to become stronger than concrete. After adding water, it pours like syrup and sets hard in 30 to 45 minutes. Use it for setting bolts, posts, handrails, machinery, fences, columns, and almost anything else to be anchored in concrete. When used outdoors, coat anchoring cement surfaces with a waterproofing masonry sealant.The 60-pound bag contains approximately a half cubic foot yield; the 7-pound pail will yield approximately 100 cubic inches.

QUIKRETE® Concrete and Asphalt Cleaner. This is a strong, acid-free, all-purpose cleaner for removing oil, grease, or soil buildup from concrete, asphalt, or any other hard surface where water can be used. Use it for brick, slate, quarry tiles, even tools and lawnmowers. QUIKRETE® Concrete and Asphalt Cleaner should also be used just prior to applications of TRAFFIC TOP® Driveway Sealer and QUIKRETE® Vinyl Concrete Patcher. Coverage will vary widely, depending on the surface texture, the amount of dirt and grease, and the thickness of the application.

QUIKRETE® Concrete Repair Caulk. This is a new, nonflammable acrylic latex caulk that dries quickly to a tough, flexible finish that blends with concrete surfaces. It can be used to repair cracks in concrete, masonry, stucco, patios, sidewalks, and driveways. QUIKRETE® Concrete Repair Caulk is more flexible and adhesive than solvent-based concrete repair products and helps prevent water and ice damage in masonry surfaces. A 10-ounce tube will caulk approximately 120 lineal feet with a 1/8" bead, or 30 lineal feet with a 1/4" bead.

QUIKRETE® Surface Coating Products

QUIKRETE® manufactures two special surface coating products, plus a stucco finish coat mix.

QUIKWALL® Surface Bonding Cement. This cement-based blend of fiberglass and fine sand allows the construction of concrete block walls without mortar joints. Simply stack blocks in position and then trowel QUIKWALL® Surface Bonding Cement on both sides over all blocks. QUIKWALL® Surface Bonding Cement can also be used in repair and renovation work as a water-resistant seal and decorative finish over existing concrete or masonry walls. Its high flexural strength makes it a better choice than concrete for some casting projects. A 50-pound bag is enough for an area of approximately 50 square feet, 1/8" thick. Special color blends are available upon request.

QUIKWALL® Fiberglass-Reinforced Foundation Coating. This fiber-reinforced material provides a protective exterior coating over below-grade exterior rigid board insulation. Applied with a heavy brush, QUIKWALL® Fiberglass-Reinforced Foundation Coating can be applied over all types of rigid insulation, including urethane, expanded polystyrene, and pressed glass fiber insulation board. The yield will depend primarily on coating thickness. A

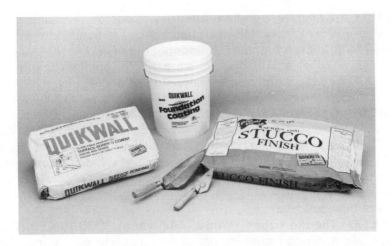

QUIKRETE® surface coating products.

40-pound bag will yield approximately 80 square feet of surface coverage in a 1/16″ coat and approximately 160 square feet in a 1/32″ coat.

QUIKRETE® Stucco Finish Coat. This product is designed for use over portland cement brown coat and scratch coat layers that have been prepared in accordance with accepted stucco procedures and methods. This material provides a beautiful white surface that accepts many textural treatments. Special color blends are available upon request. A 70-pound bag will be sufficient to do an area from 7.5 square yards to 10 square yards.

QUIKRETE® Concrete Adhesives and Fortifiers

Concrete additives and fortifiers increase concrete bond strength and workability, as well as seal pores and provide extra moisture resistance.

QUIKRETE® concrete adhesives and fortifiers.

QUIKRETE® Concrete Bonding Adhesive. Concrete bonding adhesive penetrates pores of old concrete and forms a chemical bond for new concrete toppings up to 2" thick. Roughing the old surface is usually not necessary. This product also provides a strong chemical bond for applications of plaster, stucco, gypsum plasters, and similar materials. Depending on the thickness of the application coat, a gallon will cover from 150 square feet to 300 square feet.

QUIKRETE® Concrete Acrylic Fortifier. This water-resistant acrylic resin mixture provides exceptional strength when added to QUIKRETE® cement mixes or QUIKWALL® Surface Bonding Cement. It provides a nonslip coating around pools when used with QUIKRETE® Sand Mix. It can be used to bond new toppings up to 1" thick and also strengthens and seals plaster, stucco, and masonry surfaces. A gallon will cover up to 400 square feet, depending on the thickness of the application.

QUIKRETE® Thermo-Lube® (Winter Admixture). QUIKRETE® Thermo-Lube provides antifreeze characteristics for concrete and mortar in cold weather. It also decreases setting time to prevent the moisture content from freezing and weakening structural integrity. One quart to one bag of cement at 30° F is about right, increasing as the temperature drops. At 15° F, usually 2.5 quarts per bag will be needed.

QUIKRETE® Tile-Setting Products

QUIKRETE® offers a full line of products for setting and grouting tiles, indoors and outdoors.

QUIKRETE® Thin-Set Mix. This formulation of portland cement, water-retaining chemicals, and special adhesives is used for setting tile on concrete, interior grade plywood, plaster, foam glass, gypsum wallboard, old tile surfaces, marble, gypsum plaster brown coat, and expanded polystyrene. Its

QUIKRETE® tile-setting products.

sandless mix enables those who desire to add their own sand and is a stronger vertical adhesive than sanded mixes. Coverage will vary depending on the trowel size used. A 1/4" × 1/4" square-notch trowel will cover approximately 25 square feet with a 25-pound bag.

QUIKRETE® Thin-Set Mix (Sanded). This mix is used for setting tile such as vitreous ceramic mosaics, pavers, and quarry tile on concrete, interior grade plywood, portland cement, plaster, foam glass, gypsum wallboard, old tile surfaces, marble, gypsum plaster brown coat, gypsum block, and expanded polystyrene. A 1/4" × 1/4" square-notch trowel will cover approximately 45 square feet with the yield of a 50-pound bag.

QUIKRETE® Wet Grout. This grout is used for those floor and wall tiles that require presoaking before installation, providing a hard, wear-resistant, non-shrink joint. All popular colors are available. A 25-pound bag will yield approximately enough for 200 square feet of coverage, using 4" × 4" × 1/4" tiles and 1/8" joints. Coverage will vary according to tile and joint size.

QUIKRETE® Dry Grout. The most common tiles available require no presoaking. This grout is for them. Like QUIKRETE® Wet Grout, it is available in all popular colors and forms hard, nonshrink, wear-resistant joints. A similar sized package of dry grout will have the same yield as one of wet grout.

QUIKRETE® Acid-Resistant Grout. Use this for joints between glazed and unglazed floor and wall tiles, quarry tiles, and split brick wherever exposed to mild corrosives and abrasive agents, including home cleaning detergents. It cures to a hard sanitary joint to repel water, grease, and oil. Coverage will vary depending on tile and joint size. With common 6" × 6" × 1/2" floor tile and 1/2" joints, a 50-pound bag will yield about 65 square feet of coverage.

QUIKRETE® Self-Leveling Floor Resurfacer. A self-leveling and self-finishing floor topping and underlayment, QUIKRETE® Floor Resurfacer produces a level floor ready for the installation of tile, resilient flooring, carpet, and other finishes. Use it over precast floor slabs, new concrete, weather-damaged floor slabs or poured-in-place slabs with unacceptable finishes, and existing floors; it is designed to meet the exacting specifications for installing X-ray equipment. An adhesive, such as QUIKRETE® Concrete Bonding Adhesive, must be used with it. A 50-pound bag will cover approximately 25 square feet, 1/4" thick.

QUIKRETE® Waterproofing Products

Freeze/thaw cycles and water infiltration can destroy the most carefully constructed concrete and masonry projects. But sealing with QUIKRETE® waterproofing products can protect and beautify all types of masonry.

QUIKRETE® Masonry Coating. This is a portland cement-based product used to seal and beautify porous masonry surfaces, indoors and outdoors. With nonporous surfaces, QUIKRETE® Concrete Bonding Adhesive must also be used. Simply mix with water and apply QUIKRETE® Waterproof Cement Paint over poured concrete, block, stucco, brick, or stone surfaces above or below grade. This product is excellent for dampproofing basement walls, and is available in white, gray, green, and yellow. A 20-pound bag covers an area of

QUIKRETE® waterproofing products.

up to 200 square feet, depending on the surface being coated and the amount of water added to the mix.

QUIKRETE® Heavy-Duty Masonry Coating. A powdered mix of pòrtland cement, waterproofing agents, and silica sand, this coating is minerally reinforced to provide extremely durable waterproof protection. Just add water and apply it with a brush; it works both indoors and outdoors and above or below grade. QUIKRETE® Heavy-Duty Masonry Coating can withstand extreme heat, cold, and continuous moisture. It is available in white, gray, foundation gray, yellow, and green. Maximum coverage will depend on coat thickness. At 1/16", a 40-pound bag will yield about 80 square feet; at 1/8", about 40 square feet.

QUIKRETE® Hydraulic Water-Stop Cement. This special mixture of portland cement, calcium aluminate, fine sand, and special additives sets quickly (in 5 to 10 minutes), and actually stops flowing water in 3 to 5 minutes with its characteristic expansion and high early strength. QUIKRETE® Hydraulic Water-Stop Cement is suitable for plugging leaks in masonry walls and for patching concrete basement and retaining walls, cisterns, swimming pools, fountains, etc. This material is also excellent for caulking, tuck-pointing, and repairing masonry chimneys, walls, and sills and for sealing openings around pipes and fixtures. A 66-pound bag is enough to repair approximately a 4.5 square foot area, 1" thick.

QUIKRETE® Blacktop Repair Products

Blacktop driveways, roads, parking areas, service bays, runways, walkways, tennis and basketball courts, and other play areas all require regular maintenance and repair to ensure long blacktop life.

QUIKRETE® Blacktop Patch. Use this material right out of the bag to repair chuckholes and large cracks in asphalt or concrete surfaces. QUIKRETE® Blacktop Patch is a cold mix of sand, crushed stone, and asphalt and will not

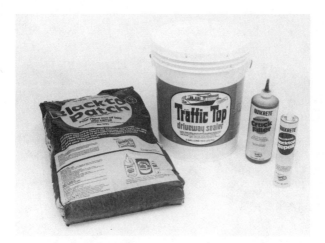

QUIKRETE® blacktop repair products.

shrink or swell, allowing the patched surface to be used immediately. No heating or curing are needed. A 66-pound bag is enough for an area of about 4.5 square feet, 1" deep.

TRAFFIC TOP® Driveway Sealer. This driveway sealer is a cold-applied coal tar pitch emulsion, fortified with oilproof rubber in latex form. It is designed to protect and beautify bituminous pavements and slabs exposed to gasoline, oil, kerosene, jet fuel, and similar petroleum products. Easily applied, it reduces pavement damage from sunlight and freeze/thaw cycles and covers up to 500 square feet with a 5-pound pail.

TRAFFIC TOP® Driveway Filler and Sealer. This heavy-duty product is slag fortified for added traction and longer life. It provides driveways with 3 to 5 years of protection from winter weather damage and salt corrosion.

QUIKRETE® Blacktop Repair Caulk. This nonflammable, weather-resistant acrylic-latex caulk offers excellent adhesion with minimal shrinkage. Use it for repairing cracks in blacktop driveways, roofs, and chimney flashings. This caulk dries quickly and blends with all types of asphalt surfaces. A 10-ounce tube will fill about 120 lineal feet using a 1/8" bead, and about 30 lineal feet with a 1/4" bead.

QUIKRETE® Driveway Crack Filler. This homogenous mix of emulsified petroleum, asphalt, latex, and other fillers is pliable in all weather and is applied right out of the container to fill cracks in concrete, asphalt, brick, woodblock, pavements, driveways, etc. Mix QUIKRETE® Driveway Crack Filler with sand for filling larger, deeper cracks. It is also an excellent expansion joint material for sidewalks, patios, driveways, or wherever new concrete abuts old installations. A gallon will cover approximately 20 lineal feet of cracks 1/2" × 2".

QUIKRETE® Specialty Products

QUIKRETE® offers many other quality products to help the home mason and do-it-yourselfer achieve professional results.

QUIKRETE® specialty products.

QUIKRETE® All-Purpose Sand. This sand is ideal for use as an underlayment base for brick patios and walks. QUIKRETE® All-Purpose Sand can also be used as a traction material on snow and ice and a ballast for winter driving. A 70-pound bag is about 3/4 cubic feet.

QUIKRETE® Play Sand. This sand is washed, dried, screened, and sterilized, and is free of organic matter. QUIKRETE® Play Sand comes in 50-pound bags and is ideal for children's sand boxes and play areas. It is also the ideal sand for building and molding. A 50-pound bag is about a half cubic foot.

QUIKBLAST® Sandblasting Sand. Sandblasting sand is available in three grades—fine, medium, and coarse—to suit every sandblasting application.

QUIKRETE® Patching Plaster. Water is all that you add to this high-quality patching material. QUIKRETE® Patching Plaster has a retarded set, allowing large quantities to be mixed at one time. This plaster actually gains strength with age, and has practically no shrinkage.

There are also QUIKRETE® cement mixes for rip rap erosion control. QUIKRETE® packages sand mix and concrete mix in biodegradable bags for use in erosion and water control projects. Use them to save time, money, labor, and machinery in the construction of headwalls and embankments, dams, and water-front bulkheads. Simply stack or lay bags in place, secure with stakes if necessary, and wet down to begin hydration. If water is not available, the cement will set up from natural moisture. For smaller jobs, lay out QUIKRETE® concrete or sand mixes in the paper packing, perforating the bags to ensure moisture penetration. A 100-square-foot wall the width of the bags requires about 170 60-pound bags.

TOOLS FOR CONCRETE AND MASONRY WORK

The tools used to finish concrete or lay brick or block are few when compared to other types of work. You probably already own a number of the tools you'll need, and you can rent, buy, or even construct the others.

Site Preparation Tools

The pickax is useful for loosening sod or soil and for digging trenches for footers. Its broad edge is very useful for working on a horizontal plane when the top layer of dirt is to be removed with minimum disturbance of the soil beneath.

A short-handled, square-faced shovel is best for handling concrete and squaring off footer trenches, etc. A tamper, such as the homemade model illustrated, is used to firm up the sides of dirt forms, post holes, slab subgrades, etc. Finally, a strong metal rake is good for leveling soil or dumped materals.

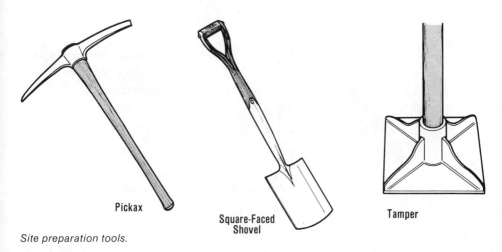

Pickax

Square-Faced
Shovel

Tamper

Site preparation tools.

Formwork Tools

You'll need a good handsaw or portable circular saw for sizing wooden forms. A 20-ounce framing hammer is best for driving larger nails, and an 8-pound sledgehammer is useful for driving in support stakes and breaking up

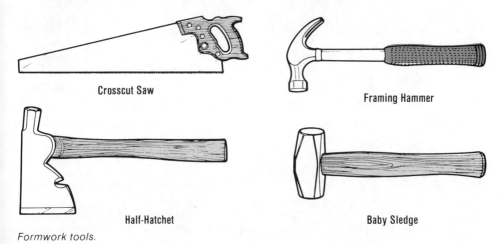

Crosscut Saw

Framing Hammer

Half-Hatchet

Baby Sledge

Formwork tools.

old concrete and brickwork. A half-hatchet is a good utility tool. The broad, sharp edge is used for pointing stakes; the hammerhead end is used for driving nails and small stakes.

Layout and Leveling Tools

A flexible tape measure, a carpenter's framing square, a 4′ level, a line level and mason's line, a chalk box, and a plumb bob are all essentials for accurately laying out the site, for setting up batter boards, and for checking forms, walls, etc., for trueness. If you plan to do several brick and block projects, a high-quality mason's level is a good investment.

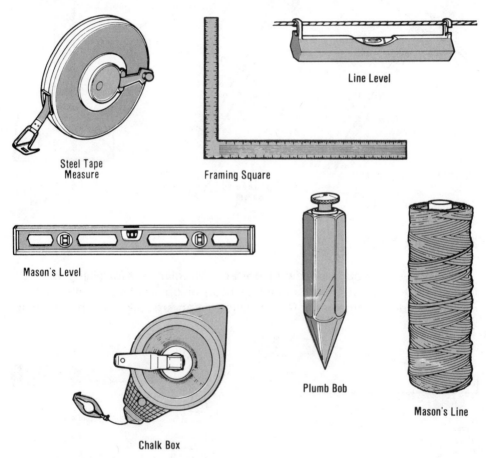

Line Level

Steel Tape
Measure

Framing Square

Mason's Level

Plumb Bob

Mason's Line

Chalk Box

Layout and leveling tools.

Mixing Tools

A sturdy wheelbarrow is ideal for mixing and transporting masonry materials and concrete. A mortar box can also be used for mixing mortar or concrete at the job site. Use the square-faced shovel or a special mortar hoe for blending together the QUIKRETE® mix and water.

For larger jobs, power mixers are by far the best way to mix concrete and mortar. Mixers of various sizes can be rented to fit the job at hand. Simply turn on the mixer, add the QUIKRETE® mix to the drum, and slowly add water. Run the mixer for three to four minutes until the concrete or mortar has reached the proper consistency. Mix only the amount of concrete you can comfortably place at one time, and mix no more mortar than you will use in a two-hour period.

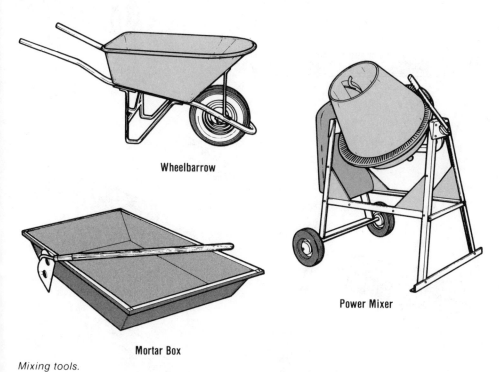

Wheelbarrow

Power Mixer

Mortar Box

Mixing tools.

Concrete Finishing Tools

Screeds or strikeboards are used to push larger pieces of aggregate below the concrete surface and level the concrete to the height of the forms. Although commercial screeds are available, a straight length of 2 × 4 lumber makes a fine screeding board. Move the board in a zigzag fashion, keeping a small roll of concrete ahead of the straightedge to fill in the low spots. The screed should be tilted in the direction of travel to obtain a cutting edge. If necessary, make a second pass to remove any remaining bumps or low spots; the screed should be tilted in the opposite direction for the second pass.

A wooden or metal hand float and a darby or long-handled bull float are used to give the concrete a uniform surface after screeding. The purpose of floating is to smooth the concrete and bring excess water to the surface. Hand floats are available in various sizes and are also quite easy to make.

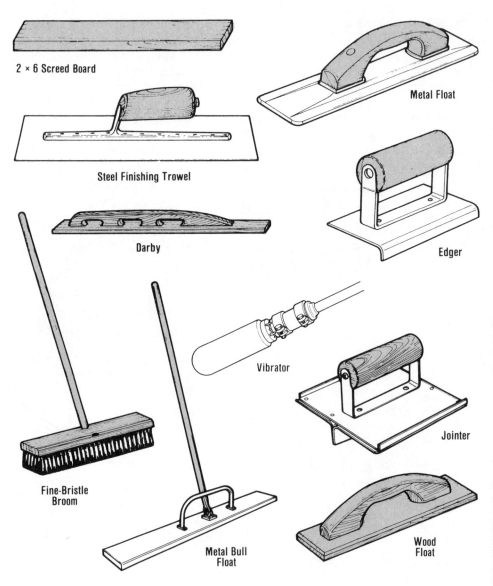

Concrete finishing tools.

Work the float over the surface using overlapping arcs. In some cases floating is the only finishing technique used. The result is a finish that is reasonably smooth with good traction. A darby is simply an oversized float that enables you to cover more area and to reach more places without having to walk on the concrete. Bull floats are larger still, and have handles so that you can work extremely large areas quickly. Quite often a bull float or darby is used prior to regular hand-floating.

Hand trowels are made of high-quality steel and are available in various sizes. They are used to produce a smooth, hard, dense finish. Never trowel a surface without floating it first—water will be trapped beneath the surface and cause the concrete to flake. Timing is critical in a troweling operation; never begin troweling until the surface water has evaporated and the concrete has lost its sheen. A surface is often troweled several times to produce the desired finish. A stiff-bristled broom is ideal for imparting a nonskid, rigid surface to floated and troweled concrete.

Edgers are used to produce a neat, rounded edge on concrete slabs, driveways, walks, and steps that will resist chipping. Edging also hardens the surface next to the form where floats are less effective. The edger is used to cut away the concrete from the form and is then run along it to compact and shape the concrete. A stainless steel edger with a 1/2" radius should be your first choice.

Jointing tools are used to cut control joints into the concrete surface. To be effective, they should extend through a quarter of the slab's depth. Such joints are needed to control cracking as the concrete expands and contracts with changing weather conditions and age. Control joints can also be cut into the concrete using a portable circular saw and masonry blade.

Internal vibrators are ideal for compacting large areas of concrete, especially when the mixture is particularly stiff. The vibrating end is attached to a reinforced hose and slowly lowered into the concrete at approximately 18" intervals along the length of the concrete. In most cases 10 to 15 seconds of vibration is sufficient to compact the concrete and remove air pockets; a thin line of mortar or paste near the vibrator indicates that it has been sufficiently worked. Do not use the vibrator to move the concrete any distance in the form.

Brickwork and Blockwork Tools

Bricklayer's trowels are available in various sizes and shapes, with the largest size being 9" to 11" long and 4" to 8" wide. Select a trowel that feels right for you, but consider that shorter, wider trowels are usually best for the beginner— since they concentrate weight nearer the wrist for less wrist strain. Trowels are used to mix mortar, to pick it up from the mortarboard, to place and spread the mortar on the brick or block, and to tap the brick or block down into the mortar bed if necessary. Pointing trowels are smaller trowels used for performing masonry repairs and tuck-pointing.

You'll also need a mortarboard or a portable hawk to hold a supply of mortar as you work. Remember to thoroughly wet down the board before beginning work so the wood does not absorb moisture from the mortar and cause it to dry out too quickly. The mortar should be kept rounded up in the center of the board and the outer edges kept clean. If spread over the board in a thin layer, the mortar will dry out quickly, and there will be a tendency for lumps to form. Proper consistency must be maintained at all times.

A brick hammer is another valuable tool. One end is shaped like a chisel and is used to smooth and shape cut bricks. The opposite end is usually square and is used for breaking bricks, striking brick set, and driving nails. Wear safety goggles whenever cutting or shaping brick.

Brick sets are also known as blocking chisels or mason's chisels. They are used to make sharp cuts on brick or to score bricks that will be broken with the

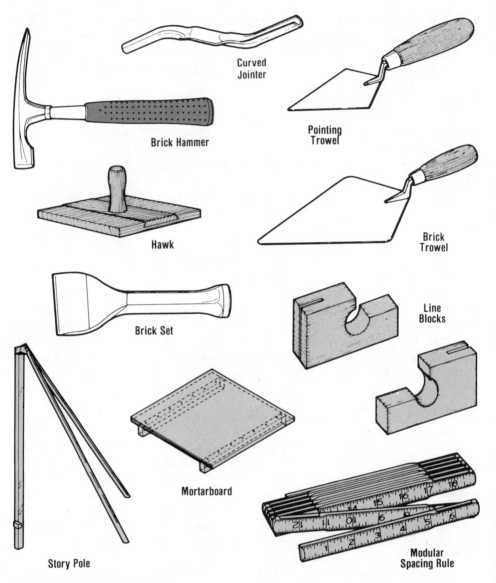

Brickwork and blockwork tools.

hammer. The handle and blade are made of a single piece of steel and measure 7″ to 8″ in overall length. The blade is 3″ to 4″ wide and is beveled to the cutting edge required. Dress the blade regularly on a grinder to keep a good cutting edge.

Line blocks are used to run a line between brick or block leads so that each course is placed accurately. Modular spacing rules and story poles are two professional tools used to more easily lay out and check the progress of brick or blockwork.

In addition to these tools, you'll need the layout and leveling tools discussed earlier.

Tool Care and Maintenance

Wheelbarrows, mortar boxes, hawks, and all concrete and masonry tools must be kept clean and free from rust. Wash all tools thoroughly in water to remove concrete and mortar before it dries. This means you'll probably have to rinse your tools several times during the workday, and give them a thorough cleaning at night. After drying them, apply a thin coat of oil to all metal surfaces to prevent rust.

BRICK

Bricks, most of which are manufactured by firing molded clay or shale, vary widely in color, texture, and size. To avoid confusion, it is best to place all brick types into one of four basic categories that are generally accepted by building supply dealers. All brick sold by reputable dealers meets the standards established for the trade.

Face Brick. Face brick is the highest quality brick available. Rigid manufacturing standards assure that texture and color will be uniform and that each brick will be nearly perfect. It will be difficult to find defects such as flaking, chipping, cracking, and warpage. This brick is commonly used for the exposed face of walls. Common colors of face brick are shades of brown, red, gray, yellow, and white.

Brick types.

Common Brick. Often called building brick, common brick is as strong as face brick but standards permit more imperfections. These bricks do not have special scorings or markings and are not produced in any special colors or textures. Common brick is generally used for backing courses in solid or cavity brick walls and for general building purposes.

Fire Brick. This brick is made of a special fire clay that will withstand the high temperatures of fireplaces, barbecues, stove liners, etc. Fire brick is generally larger than regular structural brick, and it is often hand-molded.

Patio or Paving Brick. This brick is sized for use without mortar joints and is highly resistant to cracking under great loads. It is baked for a longer period of time and, like fire brick, is made from special clays. It is used in the construction of patios and walkways.

Cored brick is available to help reduce the overall weight of the brick. Such coring does not affect the brick strength. Brick is also available with ceramic-glazed facing for easy cleaning in interior use.

Brick Grades

While brick is extremely durable, it can be damaged by freezing weather. The following three grades of brick are available that can cope with various weather conditions:

• **SW** (severe weathering) has the highest resistance to freeze/thaw and rain/freeze conditions.

• **MW** (moderate weathering) can take some rain/freeze conditions, but not severe ones.

• **NW** (no weathering) is good for use in very mild climates where no freezing or even hard frost conditions are possible.

Common brick is available in any of the three grades, while facers are manufactured to SW and MW standards only. Pavers and fire bricks are all graded SW. Your final decision on what grade to use will be dictated by local building codes and climatic conditions.

Brick Sizes

The dimensions of a United States standard building brick are 2-1/4″ × 3-3/4″ × 8″, although the actual dimensions may vary slightly because of shrinkage during baking. Actual dimensions of frequently used brick sizes are given below.

Dimensions of Commonly Used Brick	
Common	2-1/4 × 3-3/4 × 8
Modular	2-1/4 × 3-5/8 × 7-5/8
Jumbo	2-3/4 × 3-3/4 × 8
Norman	2-1/4 × 3-5/8 × 11-5/8
SCR	2-1/8 × 5-1/2 × 11-1/2
Roman	1-5/8 × 3-5/8 × 11-5/8
Baby Roman	1-5/8 × 3-5/8 × 7-5/8
Fire Brick	2-1/2 × 3-5/8 × 9
Oversize	Sizes vary with manufacturer

Nominal, or working, dimensions of the brick equal the actual dimension plus the width of the mortar joint. For example, the nominal dimension for the common 2-1/4″ × 3-3/4″ × 8″ brick using 1/2″ mortar joints would be 2-3/4″ ×

4-1/4" × 8-1/2". While common brick is usually laid up with 1/2" joints, 3/8" or 5/8" joints can also be used. Certain brick sizes, such as the modular or Roman bricks, are specifically designed to be laid up with 3/8" joints.

Buying Brick

Before selecting the exact brick you will use, visit a supplier's showroom and inspect the sample boards on hand. Various textures and colors will be displayed with a simulated mortar joint on a small panel or wall section, with mortar joints struck in popular finishes. Write down the manufacturer's identification number (also known as the range or blend number) so there is no mix-up in your order, and ask the dealer how long it will be before the bricks are available, since some bricks are made only in kiln runs at certain times of the year.

Bricks are sold singly, in cubes of 500, or by the thousand, and prices will vary according to the size of the order. Dealer delivery charges can be quite high, and for a small job the delivery charge can sometimes equal the cost of the bricks. If you can, it may pay to haul your own. But consider that the average brick weighs about 4 pounds, with a cube of 500 checking in at about a ton. So don't overload your truck.

It is also a good idea to ask the supplier whether additional bricks will be available if you run out or plan to expand your project at a future date. Some bricks are made on a limited basis and then discontinued. Finally, if you buy a cored brick, make sure that solid-end brick is available for the ends of walls, windowsills, etc.

A Word about Used Brick

Although used brick is quite popular, you must realize that it may not be structurally sound and that the units, authentic or imitation, can be more costly than new brick. Salvaged brick may have pores so permeated with impossible-to-remove mortar that a fresh mortar joint will be only 50% as strong as it should be. Old buildings contain both high-quality and low-quality bricks, and it is not likely that the salvager will sort them out. Brick manufactured a generation ago cannot compare in quality with today's brick. In short, salvaged brick is acceptable for decorative purposes and veneering but poses an unknown risk when a project must sustain loads.

CONCRETE BLOCK

Concrete block combines the strength and durability of concrete with the ease of masonry construction. And as you'll see, the use of QUIKWALL® Surface Bonding Cement allows you to lay up concrete block and brick without mortar joints. Simply stack blocks tightly in position and trowel or spray QUIKWALL® on both sides over all blocks (see pages 83 through 85 for complete details). QUIKWALL® allows the use of chipped or slightly flawed block, resulting in significantly reduced costs.

Concrete block is often used in foundation walls in home construction and for above-ground walls for garages, sheds, barns, outbuildings, and other commercial buildings. Concrete block is less expensive than other types of masonry; it is easier to build with than brick or stone; and it comes in hundreds of sizes, shapes, textures, and colors.

Sizes and Shapes

Concrete block units are made in full and half sizes and there are numerous specialty blocks for working corners, jambs, wall caps, etc. Like brick, sizes are usually referred to by their nominal dimensions, with a standard unit measur-

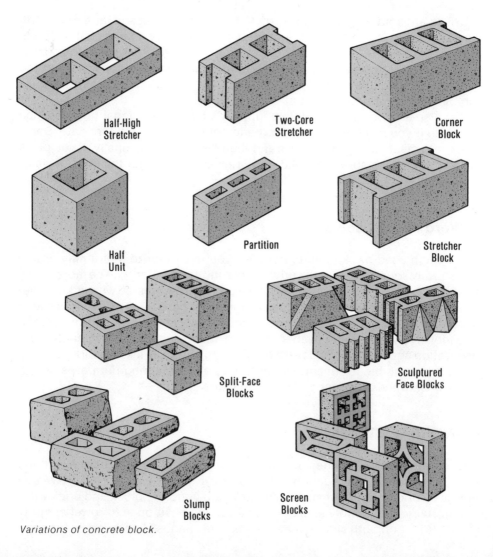

Half-High
Stretcher

Two-Core
Stretcher

Corner
Block

Half
Unit

Partition

Stretcher
Block

Split-Face
Blocks

Sculptured
Face Blocks

Slump
Blocks

Screen
Blocks

Variations of concrete block.

ing 7-5/8" wide by 7-5/8" high by 15-5/8" long referred to as 8" × 8" × 16". When laid in a wall with 3/8" mortar joints, the unit will measure exactly 16" long and 8" high. Of course, when dry-laying block for use with QUIKWALL®, the actual block dimensions will be used in planning the layout (see page 149).

Standard blocks can weigh anywhere from 25 to 50 pounds depending on the types of aggregate used in production. Lightweight blocks, often called cinder blocks, have expanded shale, clay, slate, and cinders as their aggregates. Normal-weight aggregates include sand, gravel, crushed stone, and air-cooled blast furnace slag. Most building codes require load-bearing block for foundation walls. Depending on the amount of cement used, surface texture can be coarse or smooth.

In addition to standard block, there are many other modular sizes produced. Schedule a trip to your supplier to see the full range of concrete blocks available. You'll find that some units may resemble oversized brick that is solid or cored, and that some are partially faceted so that a particular pattern results when a certain number of block is placed in a group. Depending on the area of the country, the blocks may have different names. Split block has a ready-made rustic facing, and slump block results in a rugged-looking project.

Pierced or screen block can be used to construct dividers or screens both indoors and outdoors. As a patio screen, the blocks provide a good deal of privacy with minimum blockage of air movement. Even large projects will appear light and airy. But assemblies of screen block should never be used as the major load-bearing components of a structure.

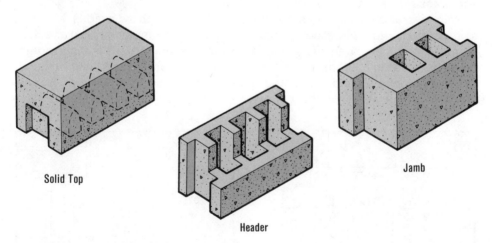

Solid Top

Header

Jamb

Special-purpose concrete block.

STONE

Natural and enduring, stone has been used as a construction material since man began building thousands of years ago. Stonework can range in appearance from the casual look of a rubblestone garden or retaining wall to the stately permanence of exactly fitted ashlar masonry. And both dry-laid and mortared constructions are possible.

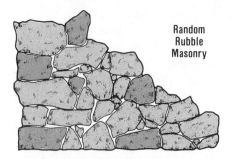

Random
Rubble
Masonry

Coursed
Rubble
Masonry

Variations of rubblestone masonry.

Types of Stone

Stone can be grouped in three broad categories. *Igneous rock,* such as granite and basalt, was formed deep in the earth from molten magma and is usually the hardest, heaviest, and most durable stone you can buy. As its name implies, *sedimentary rock,* such as sandstone and limestone, was originally formed from layers of sediment. The composition, texture, and color of these rocks can differ from place to place, but all rock of this type splits easily, making it excellent for paving and ashlar stone. The last major group, *metamorphic rock,* such as marble and slate, was formed under tremendous heat and pressure, resulting in very durable building material.

Commercial quarries and stone yards sell stone in three grades: dressed, semidressed, and undressed. Dressed stone, also commonly known as ashlar stone, is the most expensive because it is cut to specific sizes and can sometimes be ordered custom cut. It can be laid up in courses, just like bricks or concrete blocks. Semidressed and undressed stones are known as rubblestone in many areas of the country. Although semidressed stones have

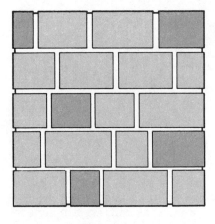

Coursed or Ranged

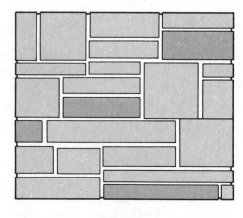

Broken Ranged

Variations of ashlar stone masonry.

Dressed

Semidressed

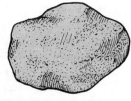
Undressed

Grades of commercially sold stone.

squared-off corners, they are not cut in specific sizes, and their edges are only roughly parallel. The cheapest grade of stone is undressed because it is neither cut nor finished; it is solid, and frequently used, just as it is found.

The larger the stone, the more quickly the work goes. Large stones fill most of the area, but the smaller ones fill in between to conserve mortar. Avoid buying stones that you cannot lift comfortably by yourself over a sustained period.

Most stone is sold by the ton, but some dealers sell it by the cubic yard. Required tonnage differs from undressed to dressed stone. One ton of rubble or undressed stone will generally cover from 25 to 45 square feet of wall, with an average thickness of 1'. One ton of dressed stone will cover approximately 50 to 60 square feet of wall surface, with an average thickness of 6". Most stone yard or quarry personnel can help you estimate how much stone is needed for a given project. Calculate the cubic footage of the area to be covered with stone and take this figure with you.

Stone should be uniform in color and texture with a good mix of sizes. If you are ordering dressed stones, specify the thicknesses you want and designate minimum and maximum lengths. Larger stones can probably be custom cut if necessary.

If you have the time, equipment, resources, and energy, you may wish to gather your own fieldstone. Fields, stream beds, and stream banks are excellent sources of fieldstone in many regions, and free stone is often available in abandoned quarries, fencelines, crumbling barn or stone foundation walls, or from building demolition contractors or road excavation crews.

Since almost all types of stone are denser, heavier, and larger than brick or block, building with stone can be difficult. The irregular shape of all but the most exactly trimmed stone can make it challenging to keep large walls plumb and true while still maintaining good bonding.

TILE, PAVERS, AND FLAGSTONE

Like brick, tile is a fire-clay product available in a wide range of sizes, textures, and shapes for both exterior and interior use. Low-fired tile is more porous and soft than the high-fired varieties, which are more vitreous (glass-like) and durable. Most tiles available today are nonporous.

Both porous and vitreous tile are available in glazed and unglazed finishes. Glazes add and intensify color, provide texture, and increase durability.

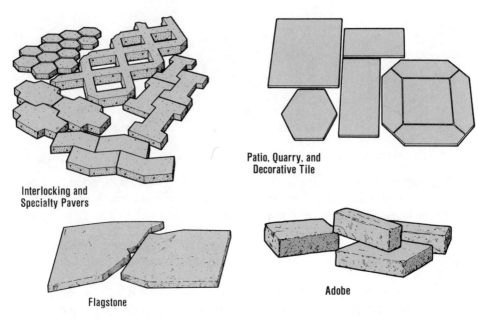

**Interlocking and
Specialty Pavers**

**Patio, Quarry, and
Decorative Tile**

Flagstone

Adobe

Paving products for indoor and outdoor use.

Glazed finishes are most often used as floor, wall, and counter coverings in kitchens, bathrooms, and interior rooms, since wet weather makes them too slippery for outdoor use. Unglazed patio or quarry tile makes an excellent nonslip surface for walkways, patios, and entertainment areas.

Both porous and vitreous tile can be set on level concrete, exterior grade plywood, portland cement, plaster, gypsum wallboard, old tile, marble, or expanded polystyrene surfaces using QUIKRETE® thin-set mixes and grouts.

For exterior work, several different construction methods can be used. Paving tile, flagstone pavers, brick, and cut stone can be set in mortar over a concrete slab. Brick, adobe, flagstone, and cut stone can also be set in a sand base, provided the subgrade is properly prepared and leveled.

PLANNING CONSIDERATIONS

Careful planning is all-important in concrete and masonry work. Paying attention to details and working carefully will make the difference between a good-looking result and one that's unsatisfactory. But remember that beauty alone won't make a project successful. It must serve a useful purpose. So the first step is to ask yourself what you want the project to do, and then you can go about finding the best way to accomplish this goal.

For example, consider a concrete slab patio. Its size is obviously an important factor. Plan 20 square feet for each person you expect to have on it at one time. Access is equally important. For a patio to function as a logical extension of the house, you must have easy access to it from an outside entrance. Climate and prevailing weather conditions also play a role in a patio's usefulness. A southern or western exposure may give you more summer sun than you'd like, and prevailing winds, rain, and winter weather may also limit the patio's usefulness.

Zoning and Building Codes

Most communities enforce zoning regulations and building codes, so if you want to construct an outbuilding, attach an addition to your home, or make any other changes to your property, obtain the necessary building permits. This is especially true in incorporated areas.

Building codes set the minimum standards for constructing a project. For example, a code may dictate the dimensions for concrete footings and acceptable methods of construction. Laws vary from place to place.

Building permits are especially important for driveways and sidewalks that cross a public way. Some cities will specify sidewalk grades when a sidewalk permit is obtained. Local codes usually spell out the "setback," which is how close to your property line you may build.

Review the deed to your property. It may include restrictive covenants or easements that will affect what you can build and where you can build it. Finally, pinpoint the locations of all underground utilities on your property such as septic systems, gas and water lines, and electric and telephone wires. Building over these utilities—or worse, striking a gas or water line during the digging of a footer—could be disastrous.

Wrong

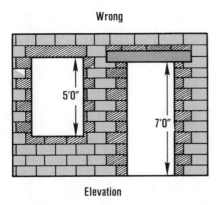

Elevation

Shaded Portion Indicates Cut Masonry

Right

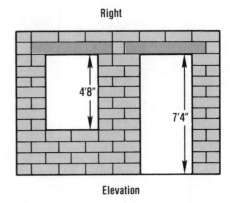

Elevation

All Masonry Full- or Half-Size Units

(Based on 8" × 8" × 16" Block)

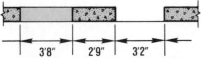
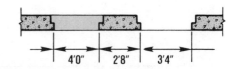

Modular planning reduces work time and material waste.

Think Modular When Planning Walls

When planning the length or height of brick or block walls, assign multiples of nominal brick or block dimensions to avoid having to cut or use half-height brick or block. The width and height of wall openings and wall areas between doors, windows, and corners should also be planned carefully to use standard full-size and half-size units. With modular planning, the work will not only be easier but the end result will look more uniform and pleasing to the eye.

To find the number of courses and the number of brick or block in each course, simply divide the proposed wall length and height by the nominal dimension of the brick or block, and then vary the figures until you can divide the number by whole brick or block vertically and by whole or half brick or block horizontally. When working with dry-stack block, remember to use the actual block dimensions in your planning. The following tables will help you estimate various wall heights and lengths when using standard-sized brick and block with typical joint sizes and dry-stack block arrangements.

Nominal Length of Concrete Masonry Walls by Stretchers

No. of Stretchers	Units 15-5/8" Long and Half Units 7-5/8" Long with 3/8" Thick Head Joints	Units 11-5/8" Long and Half Units 5-5/8" Long with 3/8" Thick Head Joints
1	1'4"	1'0"
1-1/2	2'0"	1'6"
2	2'8"	2'0"
2-1/2	3'4"	2'6"
3	4'0"	3'0"
3-1/2	4'8"	3'6"
4	5'4"	4'0"
4-1/2	6'0"	4'6"
5	6'8"	5'0"
5-1/2	7'4"	5'6"
6	8'0"	6'0"
6-1/2	8'8"	6'6"
7	9'4"	7'0"
7-1/2	10'0"	7'6"
8	10'8"	8'0"
8-1/2	11'4"	8'6"
9	12'0"	9'0"
9-1/2	12'8"	9'6"
10	13'4"	10'0"
10-/2	14'0"	10'6"
11	14'8"	11'0"
11-1/2	15'4"	11'6"
12	16'0"	12'0"
12-1/2	16'8"	12'6"
13	17'4"	13'0"
13-1/2	18'0"	13'6"
14	18'8"	14'0"
14-1/2	19'4"	14'6"
15	20'0"	15'0"
20	26'8"	20'0"

Note: Actual length of wall is measured from outside edge to outside edge of units and is equal to the nominal length minus 3/8" (one mortar joint).

Dimensions of Dry-Stacked Blocks

(Standard block units 7-5/8" × 7-5/8" × 15-5/8")

Number of Blocks	Length (Laid End to End)	Height* (Stacked)
1	1'3-5/8"	0'8"
2	2'7-1/4"	1'3-5/8"
3	3'10-7/8"	1'11-1/4"
4	5'2-1/2"	2'6-7/8"
5	6'6-1/8"	3'2-1/2"
6	7'9-3/4"	3'10-1/8"
7	9'1-3/8"	4'5-3/4"
8	10'5"	5'1-3/8"
9	11'8-5/8"	5'9"
10	13'1/4"	6'4-5/8"
12	15'7-1/2"	7'7-7/8"
15	19'6-3/8"	9'6-3/4"

*Includes 3/8" mortar bed, first course only.
Note: Approximately 56 blocks are required per 50 square feet of wall. One 50-lb. bag of QUIK-WALL® fiberglass mix covers 50 square feet with a 1/8" coating.

Nominal Height of Concrete Masonry Walls by Courses

No. of Courses	Units 7-5/8" High and 3/8" Thick Bed Joint	Units 3-5/8" High and 3/8" Thick Bed Joint
1	8"	4"
2	1'4"	8"
3	2'0"	1'0"
4	2'8"	1'4"
5	3'4"	1'8"
6	4'0"	2'0"
7	4'8"	2'4"
8	5'4"	2'8"
9	6'0"	3'0"
10	6'8"	3'4"
15	10'0"	5'0"
20	13'4"	6'8"
25	16'8"	8'4"
30	20'0"	10'0"
35	23'4"	11'8"
40	26'8"	13'4"
45	30'0"	15'0"
50	33'4"	16'8"

Note: For concrete masonry units 7-5/8" and 2-5/8" in height laid with 3/8" mortar joints. Height is measured from center to center of mortar joint.

Nominal Heights of Common Brick Walls Using 1/2" Mortar Joints

Courses	Height
1	0'2-3/4"
2	0'5-1/2"
3	0'8-1/4"
4	0'11"
5	1'1-3/4"
6	1'4-1/2"
7	1'7-1/4"
8	1'10"
9	2'0-3/4"
10	2'3-1/2"
11	2'6-1/4"
12	2'9"
13	2'11-3/4"
14	3'2-1/2"
15	3'5-1/4"
16	3'8"
17	3'10-3/4"
18	4'1-1/2"
19	4'4-1/4"
20	4'7"
21	4'9-3/4"
22	5'0-1/2"
23	5'3-1/4"
24	5'6"
25	5'8-3/4"
26	5'11-1/2"
27	6'2-1/4"
28	6'5"
29	6'7-3/4"
30	6'10-1/2"
31	7'1-1/4"
32	7'4"
33	7'6-3/4"
34	7'9-1/2"
35	8'0-1/4"
36	8'3"
37	8'5-3/4"
38	8'8-1/2"
39	8'11-1/4"
40	9'2"
41	9'4-3/4"
42	9'7-1/2"
43	9'10-1/4"
44	10'1"
45	10'3-3/4"
46	10'6-1/2"
47	10'9-1/4"
48	11'0"
49	11'2-3/4"
50	11'5-1/2"
51	11'8-1/4"
52	11'11"
53	12'1-3/4"
54	12'4-1/2"
55	12'7-1/4"
56	12'10"
57	13'0-3/4"
58	13'3-1/2"
59	13'6-1/4"
60	13'9"

Calculating Concrete Volume

Concrete is measured by volume, usually in cubic feet or cubic yards (27 cubic feet). Calculate the total amount of concrete required by using the following formula:

$$\frac{\text{Width (feet)} \times \text{Length(feet)} \times \text{Thickness (inches)}}{12} = \text{cubic feet}$$

For example, a 3'-wide sidewalk that is 24' long and 4" thick would require 24 cubic feet of concrete.

$$\frac{3' \times 24' \times 4''}{12} = 24 \text{ cubic feet}$$

To be safe, add 10% to this estimate to account for spills, uneven subgrades, and so on. This additional 10% would bring the total to about 26.4 cubic feet or just about a cubic yard of concrete.

QUIKRETE® Concrete, Mortar, and Sand Mixes are available in three bag sizes: 80-pound (2/3, or 0.66 cubic foot), 60-pound (1/2, or 0.50 cubic foot), and 40-pound (1/3, or 0.33 cubic foot). These are approximate yields that apply in most areas of the country. However, in certain areas, the yields will vary considerably due to the nature of aggregates available to local manufacturers.

To determine the number of bags needed for a project, divide the number of cubic feet to be placed by the cubic foot yield of the bag size being used, applying the following formulas:

Decimals

$$\text{(cubic feet in bag)} \sqrt{\text{(cubic feet of coverage)}}$$

Ratios

$$\frac{\text{(cubic feet of coverage)}}{1} \times \text{(cubic feet in bag)}$$

In the example above, if 80-pound packages of mix were used, 40 bags would be needed.

Decimals

$$.66\sqrt{\begin{array}{r} 40. \\ \overline{26.40.} \\ \underline{26\ 4} \\ 00 \end{array}}$$

Ratios

$$\frac{26.4}{1} \times \frac{3^*}{2} = \frac{79.2}{2} = \frac{39.6}{1}$$

*Note: In dividing ratios, the calculation proceeds as multiplication after inverting the numerator and denominator of the divisor. Thus, the 2/3 cubic foot yield of an 80-pound bag becomes 3/2 in applying the formula.

When estimating concrete needs for steps, consider each individual step as an individual slab. In the example shown here, the bottom step will need 7-2/3

No. of Stretchers	Units 8″ Long and Half Units 4″ Long with 1/2″ Thick Head Joints	Units 11-5/8″ Long and Half Units 5-5/8″ Long with 3/8″ Thick Head Joints
	Nominal Length of Concrete Brick Walls by Stretchers	
1	8-1/2″	1′0″
1-1/2	1′1″	1′6″
2	1′5″	2′0″
2-1/2	1′9-1/2″	2′6″
3	2′1-1/2″	3′0″
3-1/2	2′6″	3′6″
4	2′10″	4′0″
4-1/2	3′2-1/2″	4′6″
5	3′6-1/2″	5′0″
5-1/2	3′11″	5′6″
6	4′3″	6′0″
6-1/2	4′7-1/2″	6′6″
7	4′11-1/2″	7′0″
7-1/2	5′4″	7′6″
8	5′8″	8′0″
8-1/2	6′1/2″	8′6″
9	6′4-1/2″	9′0″
9-1/2	6′9″	9′6″
10	7′1″	10′0″
10-/2	7′5-1/2″	10′6″
11	7′9-1/2″	11′0″
11-1/2	8′2″	11′6″
12	8′6″	12′0″
12-1/2	8′10-1/2″	12′6″
13	9′2-1/2″	13′0″
13-1/2	9′7″	13′6″
14	9′11″	14′0″
14-1/2	10′3-1/2″	14′6″
15	10′7-1/2″	15′0″
20	14′2″	20′0″

cubic feet while the top step requires 6 cubic feet for a total of 13-2/3 cubic feet of concrete without a loss factor.

For circles or cylindrical forms, multiply the square of the radius by 3.1416 by the height.

For quick estimates of slab and step work, use the table on page 152.

Estimating Brick and Block

To find the number of brick or block needed for a wall, multiply the number of units in each course by the number of courses and subtract the appropriate amounts for window, door, and wall openings. If building a double wythe brick wall, multiply this number by two. Adjust this number if any special bond patterns are being used, such as bull headers to tie together a double wythe wall.

When working with block, remember to determine the number of corner, capping, and other specialty blocks you will need. In many cases, it is wise to sketch out your plans to scale on a piece of graph paper. While they need not

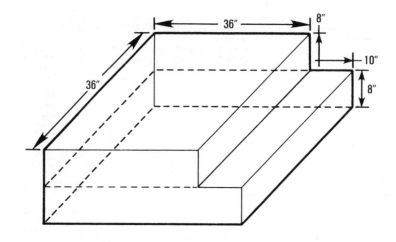

Break down larger projects into easy-to-understand units when estimating concrete needs.

QUIKRETE® Concrete Mix Required to Pour a Concrete Slab*											
Area in Square Feet	2	3	5	7	9	15	20	35	45	50	100
Slab 4" thick — 60-lb. bags	1-1/3	2	3-1/3	4-2/3	6	10	13-1/3	23-1/3	30	33-1/3	66-2/3
Slab 4" thick — 80-lb. bags	1	1-1/2	2-1/2	3-1/2	4-1/2	7-1/2	10	17-1/2	22-1/2	25	50
Slab 6" thick — 60-lb. bags	2	3	5	7	9	15	20	35	45	50	100
Slab 6" thick — 80lb. bags	1-1/2	2-1/4	3-3/4	5-1/4	6-3/4	11-1/4	15	26-1/4	33-3/4	37-1/2	75

QUIKRETE® Sand Mix Required for a 1" Topping*											
Area in Square Feet	2	3	5	7	9	15	20	35	45	50	100
60-lb. bags	1/3	1/2	5/6	1-1/5	1-1/2	2-1/3	3-1/3	6	7-1/2	8-1/3	16-2/3
80-lb. bags	1/4	3/8	5/8	7/8	1-1/8	2-7/8	2-1/2	4-3/8	5-5/8	6-1/4	12-1/2

*Does not allow for losses due to uneven subgrade, spillage, etc. Add an additional 5% to 10% to figures listed.
Note: These are approximate yields that apply in most areas of the country. In certain areas the yields will vary considerably due to the nature of aggregates available to local manufacturers.

be elaborate, such drawings help you visualize the project, estimate materials, and spot any design flaws or trouble spots before work begins.

Determining Mortar Requirements

The following chart lists the number of bags of QUIKRETE® Mortar Mix required to lay 2-1/4" × 3-3/4" × 8" common brick using 3/8" mortar joints. When using 1/2" mortar joints, increase the amount of mix by 1/3; when using 5/8" joints, increase the mix amount by 2/3 the quantities stated.

Concrete block is normally laid up using 3/8" joints.

QUIKRETE® Mortar Mix Required to Lay Bricks*
8″ × 2″ × 4″ with 3/8″ Joints

Number of Bricks	50	65	100	150	200	250	300	400	500	750	1000
60-lb. bags	1	1-1/3	2	3	4	5	6	8	10	15	20
80-lb. bags	3/4	1	1-1/2	2-1/3	3	4	4-2/3	6	7-1/2	11-1/2	15-1/3

*In building a wall, approximately 6-1/2 bricks 8″ × 2″ × 4″ laid with 3/8″ joints are required per square foot. In paving a walk or floor, approximately 4-1/3 bricks 8″ × 4″ × 3/8″ joints are required per square foot.
Note: These are approximate yields that apply in most areas of the country. In certain areas the yields will vary considerably due to the nature of aggregates available to local manufacturers.

QUIKRETE® Mortar Mix Required to Lay Blocks*
8″ × 16″ × 8″ with 3/8″ Joints

Number of Blocks	20	27	40	80	100	200	300	400	500	750	1000
60-lb. bags	1	1-1/3	2	4	5	10	15	20	25	37-1/2	50
80-lb. bags	3/4	1	1-1/2	3	3-3/4	7	11	15	18-1/2	28	37

*In building a wall, approximately one block 8″ × 16″ × 8″ laid with 3/8″ joints is required per square foot.
Note: These are approximate yields that apply in most areas of the country. In certain areas the yields will vary considerably due to the nature of aggregates available to local manufacturers.

CURING CONCRETE

Curing is one of the most important steps in concrete construction. Proper curing increases the strength and durability of concrete, and a poor curing job can ruin an otherwise well-done project. Proper water content and temperature are essential for good curing. In near-freezing temperatures, the hydration process slows considerably. When weather is too hot, dry, or windy, water is lost by evaporation from the concrete, and hydration stops, resulting in finishing difficulties and cracks. The ideal circumstances for curing are ample moisture and moderate temperature and wind conditions.

Moist-curing is done in several ways: by covering the surface with wet burlap; by keeping the surface wet with a lawn sprinkler; or by sealing the concrete surface with plastic sheeting, waterproof paper, or curing compound to prevent moisture loss.

If burlap is used, it should be free of chemicals that could weaken or discolor the concrete. New burlap should be washed before use. Place it when the concrete is hard enough to withstand surface damage and sprinkle it periodically to keep the concrete surface continuously moist.

Water curing with lawn sprinklers, nozzles, or soaking hoses must be continuous to prevent interruption of the curing process.

Curing with plastic sheets is convenient. They must be laid flat, thoroughly sealed at joints, and anchored carefully along edges. But curing with plastic can cause patchy discoloration in colored concrete. For colored concrete chemical curing compounds are recommended.

Pigmented curing compounds provide the easiest and most convenient method of curing. These compounds are applied by spraying soon after the final finishing operation. The surface should be damp, but not wet. Complete coverage is essential.

Use of curing compounds is not recommended during late fall in northern climates on surfaces where deicers will be used to melt ice and snow. Using curing compounds at that time may prevent proper air-drying of the concrete, which is necessary to enhance its resistance to damage caused by deicers.

Curing should be started as soon as possible and should continue for a period of five days in warm weather (70° F or higher) or seven days in cooler weather (50° F to 70° F). The temperature of the concrete must not be allowed to fall below 50° F during the curing period.

Working in Cold and Hot Weather

Ideally, concrete work should be done well in advance of cold weather. When placed during temperate weather, it is not necessary to take special precautions to prevent the subgrade and concrete from freezing, and there is sufficient time for the concrete to develop strength to resist freezing and thawing and chemical deicers. However, a good concrete job can be done in colder weather if the correct methods are carefully followed.

Do not place concrete on frozen ground. Straw mats, loose straw coverings, and similar materials can be used to keep the earth from freezing prior to pouring the concrete. Check over the site and forms, and remove any accumulation of frost or ice.

Remember, proper hardening of concrete occurs when the temperature of the mix falls between 50° F and 70° F. If the temperature falls below 50° F, you should heat the mixing water or use hot water from a garden hose.

When there is danger of freezing, concrete should be kept warm during curing. Insulating blankets, or 12" to 24" of dry straw, covered with canvas, waterproof paper, or plastic sheeting to keep it dry and in place, can be used. The effectiveness of the protection can be checked by placing a thermometer under the covering. Slab edges and corners are most vulnerable to freezing.

QUIKRETE® Thermo-Lube is a calcium-base liquid with special rust inhibitors that is added to concrete and mortar during cold weather to help accelerate the set before freezing can occur.

In very hot weather, steps must be taken to keep the concrete sufficiently cool and to prevent rapid loss of surface moisture: (1) dampen the subgrade and forms before pouring; (2) minimize the finishing time required by having sufficient manpower on hand; (3) erect sunshades and windbreaks; (4) use temporary coverings, such as wet burlap or plastic sheeting, during the finishing procedure; (5) use light mist sprays periodically to prevent excessive evaporation from the concrete; and (6) start the curing process as soon as possible, using continuous wet methods or white pigmented curing compounds. During very hot, dry weather, plan to place and finish concrete during the cooler, early morning or late evening hours.

GLOSSARY

Adhesion. The sticking together of substances that are in contact with one another.

Admixtures. All materials, other than portland cement, water, and aggregates, that are added to concrete, mortar, or grout immediately before or during mixing.

Aggregate. Bulk materials, such as sand, gravel, crushed stone, slag, pumice, and scoria, that are used in making concrete.

Anchor Bolts. Any of a variety of rather large J- or L-shaped bolts designed to have a portion embedded in concrete or mortar.

Ashlar. A squared or rectangular block of building stone. A wall made of squared building stones in the ashlar pattern.

Backfilling. The process of piling earth against the outer surface of a form.

Base Coat. Each of the lower layers of plaster, if more than one coat is applied.

Batter Boards. A board frame supported by stakes set back from the corners of a structure that allows for relocating certain points after excavation. Saw kerfs in the boards indicate the location of the edges of the footings and the structure being built.

Bed Joint. The horizontal layer of mortar on which a masonry unit is laid.

Block. A concrete masonry unit made with fine aggregate and cement that is shaped in a mold. Any of a variety of shaped light- or standard-weight masonry units.

Bond. The property of a hardened mortar that knits the masonry units together; also, the lapping of brick in a wall.

Brick Masonry. A type of construction that has units of baked clay or shale of uniform size, small enough to be placed with one hand, laid in courses with mortar joints to form walls of virtually unlimited length and height.

Brick Set. A wide-blade chisel used for cutting bricks and concrete blocks.

Brown Coat. The second coat of plaster or stucco in three-coat work.

Buttered. The small end of a brick that has a quantity of mortar placed onto it (e.g., the act of buttering a brick's end with mortar).

Caulk. To seal up crevices with some flexible material.

Closure Brick. A partial brick that is cut to fit into a place to complete a course.

Coloring Agents. Colored aggregates or mineral oxides ground finer than cement.

Concrete. An artificial stone made by mixing cement and sand with gravel, broken stone, or other aggregate. These materials must be mixed with sufficient water to cause the cement to set and bind the entire mass.

Control Joints. Continuous vertical joints built into concrete walls to control cracking resulting from unusual stresses. The joints are intended to permit slight wall movement without cracking.

Coping. A brick, block, stone, or concrete cap placed at the top of a masonry wall to prevent moisture from falling directly on it and weakening the wall.

Corbeling. Courses of brick set out beyond the face of a wall in order to form a self-supporting projection.

Courses. One of the continuous horizontal layers (rows) of masonry that form the masonry structure.

Curing. The process of protecting concrete against loss of moisture during the earlier stages of setting.

Dry Mixture. A mixture of concrete whose water content is severely restricted.

Edger. A concrete finishing tool for rounding and smoothing edges, which strengthens them.

Edging. The process of rounding the edge of freshly poured concrete; one of several finishing techniques.

Efflorescence. A powdery stain, usually white, on the surface of or between masonry units. It is caused by the leaching of soluble salts to the surface.

Expansion Joint. A material placed within or a scoring of the concrete that allows it to expand without cracking.

Exposed Aggregate. A concrete finish achieved by embedding aggregate into the surface, allowing the concrete to set up somewhat, then hosing down and brushing away the concrete covering the top portion of the aggregate.

Face Brick. A type of brick made specifically for covering (veneering) walls.

Finish Coat. The top layer of plaster if the plaster is applied in more than one coat.

Flashing. The waterproofing covering placed at certain points in brick masonry to hold back water or to direct any moisture outside of the wall.

Float. A wooden tool used to finish a concrete surface.

Footing. A base for a wall or other structure that provides stability for that structure.

Form. A parameter or set of parameters made from earth or wood and, on occasion, steel, that contains the footing concrete.

Frost Line. The maximum depth to which frost normally penetrates the soil during the winter. This depth varies from area to area depending on the climate.

Furrowing. Striking a V-shaped trough in a bed of mortar.

Gradation. The distribution of particle sizes, from coarse to fine, in a given sample of fine or coarse aggregate.

Grout. A water-cement, or water-cement-sand mixture, used to plug holes or cracks in concrete, seal joints, fill spaces between machinery bed plates and concrete foundations, and for similar plugging or sealing purposes.

Hawk. A fairly small board with a handle beneath it that is used for holding mortar.

Header. A masonry unit laid flat with its longest dimensions perpendicular to the face of the wall. It is generally used to tie two wythes of masonry together.

Hydration. The chemical reaction that occurs when water is added to cement, causing it to harden.

Joint. Any place where two or more edges or surfaces come to a union.

Jointer. A tool used for making grooves or control joints in concrete surfaces to control cracking. (See **Control Joint.**)

Lintel. A beam placed over an opening in a wall.

Masonry. A construction made of prefabricated masonry units laid in various ways and joined together with mortar.

Mixers. Vehicles or containers used to blend or mix the ingredients of concrete.

Moisture Content. The amount of water contained within the aggregate used in concrete.

Mortar. A mixture of cement, sand, and water without coarse aggregate. It is used chiefly for bonding masonry units together.

Pavers. Bricks in numerous sizes and shapes that are used in constructing sidewalks, patios, and driveways.

Pier. A free-standing column.

Pilaster. A projection from a masonry wall that provides strength for the wall.

Plasticity Consistency. A sluggish flow without segregation.

Plumb. That which is vertically perpendicular as measured with a spirit level or plumb bob.

Pointing. The process of inserting mortar into horizontal and vertical joints after a masonry unit has been laid.

Portland Cement. A number of types of cement with unique characteristics manufactured from limestone and mixed with shale, clay, or marl.

Precast Concrete. Any concrete member that is cast in forms at a place other than its final position of use.

Pre-Mix. Any of several packaged mixtures of ingredients used for preparing concrete or mortar.

Reinforcing Rod. A steel rod that is used for reinforcing concrete and masonry structures.

Retaining Wall. A wall that is constructed to hold soil in place.

Rowlock. A brick laid on its edge (face).

Rubble. Rough fragments of broken stone either naturally formed or quarried; used in masonry.

Running Bond. This is the same as common bond, with continuous horizontal joints, but the vertical joints are offset or in line.

Scratch Coat. The first coat of plaster or stucco.

Screed. A long, very straight board used for striking off concrete.

Screeding. The process of leveling the surface of a concrete slab by striking off the excess concrete.

Segregation. The tendency of particles of the same size in a given mass of aggregate to gather together whenever the material is being loaded, transported, or otherwise disturbed.

Set. The process during which mortar or concrete hardens. Initial set occurs when the concrete has to be broken to change its shape, generally about an hour after it is placed. Final set occurs generally about 10 hours after placing the concrete.

Shell. The sides and recessed ends of a concrete block.

Soldier. A brick laid on its end so that its longest dimension is parallel to the vertical axis of the face of the wall.

Stretcher. A masonry unit laid flat with its longest dimension parallel to the face of the wall.

Striking Off. The process of removing excess concrete to a level needed.

Stucco. A finish composed of two or more layers of mortar (white or colored) that is applied to either indoor or outdoor walls.

Tamp. The process of compacting concrete with rakes or short lengths of lumber.

Texturizing. Creating a particular finish, such as brushed, smoothed, etched, or pockmarked.

Ties. A wire, rod, or snap that is used to hold wall forms at a specific separation.

Trowel. A steel tool with a flat surface that causes a concrete surface to become very smooth.

Tuck-Pointing. The process of refilling old joints with new mortar.

Veneer. A layer of bricks or stones that serves as a facing.

Wales. Horizontal members that aid in wall/form reinforcement and distribution of forces.

Weep Holes. The openings made in mortar joints that facilitate drainage of built-up moisture.

Wire Mesh. Any of a variety of types of bonded wire forming a mat used to reinforce slabs of concrete.

Workability. The ease or difficulty of placing and consolidating concrete.

Wythe. A vertical stack of bricks one thickness wide (e.g., a veneer course).

INDEX